Readers say:

"*Crucified Woman* says some very important things about how women are feeling and thinking theologically, and it focuses these concerns in the sculpture that gives the book its title. It will certainly precipitate lots of dialogue."

Lois Wilson

"I loved it. Both recording a historical event, and drawing out its significance so well for art, theology, social justice, pastoral concern, and the pain of women caught in what we've told them God is like.... Questions are planted, like insistent seeds, on every page. Patriarchy will never be the same!"

Bruce McLeod

"The *Crucified Woman* is an excellent introduction to feminist theology addressed to a wide audience in the United Church....I thought it was a wonderful idea to use the various responses to the statue as an entry into theological reflection ... I enjoyed the book."

Gregory Baum

"This is a marvellous book. It takes a particular incident and uses it as a point of departure for some very relevant reflection. The style and construction of the book is elegant and accessible. It makes an important contribution to a crucial discussion in and for the churches. I imagine it being used in study groups and courses for many years to come. I look forward to its publication."

Mary Jo Leddy

Crucified Woman

Doris
Jean
Dyke

THE UNITED CHURCH PUBLISHING HOUSE

Grateful acknowledgement is made for permission to reprint from copyrighted material, including the following:

From "Christa" by Michael J. Farrell in *National Catholic Reporter*. Reprinted by permission, *National Catholic Reporter*, P.O. Box 419281, Kansas City, MO 64141.

From *The Fire Dwellers* by Margaret Laurence. Used by permission of the Canadian Publishers, McClelland & Stewart, Toronto.

From "The Merchant of Heaven" in *The Tomorrow Tamer* by Margaret Laurence. Used by permission of the Canadian Publishers, McClelland & Stewart, Toronto.

From "Reflections on the Christa" by Edwina Hunter in the *Journal of Women and Religion*, Centre for Women and Religion, 2400 Ridge Road, Berkeley California 94709. Reprinted by permission.

From *The Memoirs of a Survivor* by Doris Lessing (Octagon Press, London). Reprinted by permission.

Canadian Cataloguing in Publication Data

Dyke, Doris Jean, 1930 -
    Crucified woman

Includes bibliographical references.
ISBN 0-919000-68-1

1. Church and social problems - Canada -
Protestant churches. 2. Christian art and
symbolism - Canada. 3. Body, Human - Religious
aspects - Protestant churches. 4. Feminism -
Religious aspects - Christianity. I. Title.

HN39.C2D8 1991   261'.1'0971   C91-0945519-5

The United Church Publishing House
85 St. Clair Avenue East
Toronto, Ont.
M4T 1M8

Publisher: R.L. Naylor
Editor-in-Chief: Peter Gordon White
Editorial Assistant: Elizabeth Phinney
Book Design: Laura Ciruls, Dept. of Graphics and Print
Cover Illustration: Kelley Aitken
Printed in Canada by: Best/Gagné Book Manufacturers
5 4 3 2   92 93 94 95

For Catherine Anne Jane

Once mother and child;
now women together.

Contents

Author's Note

This book is about restored relationships, healing, and justice, which are all the same thing. When we reflect on what our life is about, one answer is that we should care for each other and for all of creation.

Social justice concerns within the church and society are usually seen as quite different pursuits from those of pastoral ministry, which are identified with the work of caring for individuals and families. I believe that caring for the world through social justice is not different from caring for individuals. The common good brings about personal well-being. If women are to be cared for they need not only healing but also the prevention of needless suffering.

The responses of people to the presence of the sculpture *Crucified Woman* in Toronto, Canada, at Bloor Street United Church and Emmanuel College, a theological college of The United Church of Canada, are used as a way into theological reflections on Protestantism and art, the female body, and the needless suffering of women. What emerges does not belong exclusively in any one category that has been designed to organize theology. The theological reflection as it is offered in this book is collaborative and suggestive, narrative and personal. It is a theology of liberation, which is existential, biblical, and concerned with process – both social change and healing.

There are two reasons for including comments made by others. In the first place the theology that emerged did so *in community*, and I want to use the words of the people who spoke them. It is as if the sculpture invited viewers to engage in their own struggles with the Christian faith as they have received it and understood it. Comments do not necessarily conform to the traditional disciplinary norms of theology. Only direct quotations can catch the variety and the urgency of the work of the people. Related to the need of persons, mostly women, to talk about their lives in relation to the Christian story, the comments illustrate the way that the sculpture uncovers layers of theological thinking and enables change and growth. The second reason for including so many comments is that, for many women, the story of the *Crucified Woman* is a transforming story, a salvation story, promising a future unlike the past.

The connection between our faith and our stories is one of the ways of seeing the relationship between Christ and our lives. The sculpture connected the lives that women lead with the Christian story – some said for the first time, others said "once again."

The style of the book is personal and conversational. Details are often included because they contribute to the whole – like the pieces in a patch-work quilt. It is important that the gardener at Emmanuel College landscaped the area around the sculpture carefully and that the security personnel protected it from vandalism. Exclusive preoccupation with the preparation and serving of food, though valuable in and of itself, has often prevented women from participating in the common life in other ways. Parts of the book discuss such ambiguities and illustrate the importance of how food is provided at communal events, as well as how food is used as a religious symbol and how shared bread becomes Christ with us. While acknowledging that many women want to move towards more independence and autonomy, I think it is important that men should be encouraged towards a more connected and caring life. It is also important to value the work that has been done traditionally by women.

Toronto is a multi-religious city. I have been moved by the understanding and appreciation of the sculpture by persons of religious traditions other than Christian, as well as by those who call themselves post-Christian. Art, created as it is out of the culture in which we live, is a way of connecting us across cultural and religious barriers. In some strange way we value the art of others and come closer by understanding each other.

Christian feminists are often asked why they stay in the church. My own answer to that question is to be found in this book. I know that the book is controversial. I have tried to honour the theological reasons of those who oppose the sculpture by quoting their words, but I have not heightened the argument, because I do not think that only disagreement is newsworthy.

I hope the reader will hear my voice and the voices of others. I expect that these stories will help you to remember some of your own stories, because it is through story that we come to know God, ourselves, and others.

Lent 1991

Acknowledgements

Some of the ideas in this book might have been written in another context, but this book would not have been written without the sculpture *Crucified Woman,* so my first thank you is to Almuth Lutkenhaus-Lackey, the artist whose work has been so important to many people and especially to me. The title of the book belongs to her: she named the sculpture before she started work on it.

My next thank you goes to my friend Johan Aitken, who first told the arts committee of Bloor Street United Church about the sculpture, arranged for us to see it, and who first imagined it in the chancel.

Deep appreciation goes to Clifford Elliott, who was involved in all of the decisions and discussions and also moderated the controversy at Bloor Street Church with energy, compassion, and theological ability. Those who were members of the arts committee at that memorable time accomplished more than we anticipated. I am grateful to the people in the congregation who offered the responses that I have recorded and reflected upon.

Others whom I want to name were significant participants either at Bloor Street Church or at Emmanuel College: Beth Robinson, Lynn McDonald, B.J. Klassen, John Klassen, Gary Redcliffe, Roger Hutchinson, Jan Bush, Helga Kutz Harder, Joan Wyatt, Alexandra Caverly-Lowery, Douglas Jay, Nancy Newman, the late David Newman, Ted Reeve, Mary Reeve, Cathy Short, Carol Gierak, and the late Margaret Laurence.

Dodie Smith joyfully and carefully transferred the manuscript onto computer disk, caring so deeply about the sculpture and this work that she herself became a part of the story.

Nancy Jackman aided generously in the publication of the book. Peter Gordon White, a delightfully creative editor, managed to be imaginative and realistic at the same time. Rosemary Grant willingly took on the work of photographing the sculpture. Elizabeth Phinney edited energetically, intelligently, and with good humour.

Lillian Perigoe, my colleague, and Mary Horney, friend of a lifetime, gave careful reading and made many suggestions.

Catherine Evans, my daughter, read and reread each chapter. Always generous with intellectual and emotional support, her good judgement led to many improvements.

Donald Milne, my husband, whose love, wisdom, and good humour support me at all times, was especially encouraging at this unusually single-minded time in my life.

Sometimes as I was writing, I thought of my mother Cassie McFadden Scott. She would have loved the sculpture and this story. She died the year the sculpture was created.

Some of the ideas in this book were first expressed in my article under the same title in the *Toronto Journal of Theology*, Volume 5, Number 2, 1989.

Chapter One

Celebration and Controversy: In the Church

A sculpture, *Crucified Woman*, stands outdoors on the grounds of Emmanuel College, a theological college of The United Church of Canada in the University of Toronto. It was a gift to the college by the artist who created it, Almuth Lutkenhaus-Lackey. In its garden setting, surrounded by silver birches, junipers, and scarlet flowering annuals, it is both startling and peaceful.

The sculpture has evoked controversy and criticism, as well as reflection and celebration. Theologians argue about it, and women write poetry. Wedding and graduation photos are taken beside it. Art students, theology students, and high school students, clipboards in hand, request interviews and write essays about it. Tourists come with by with cameras and want to know more. Some people stand in silence, others engage in passionate conversation. Often a bouquet of flowers can be seen on or near the sculpture, fresh, wilted, or frozen; more visible in the winter than in the summer – like the sculpture itself.

Some people do not like the sculpture and look away;

others shrug or laugh nervously. Outdoors, the sculpture is accessible to everyone, but it is in the back garden, so most who see it have come looking for it. It has become a place for women to come alone or in community to remember the lives of each other and those who have gone before. In December 1989, hundreds gathered around the *Crucified Woman* in anguish on the day after the massacre of fourteen female engineering students in Montreal. It draws the sorrows of women. It is a place where women know that their suffering is gathered up into the suffering of Christ.

Controversy about the sculpture indicates its timeliness. Thirty years ago it might have been unthinkable; today it is unavoidable. The sculpture was completed in 1976. In 1979, it was hung in the chancel of Bloor Street United Church in Toronto as a focus for Passiontide services and Easter. In 1986, it was given to Emmanuel College. At both Emmanuel College and Bloor Street United Church, it caused controversy, healing, and change. Women saw their suffering, their dying, and their resurrection embodied in a woman's body. People were able to see the particularity of this image and see beyond it. The story of the sculpture *Crucified Woman* is a story of change and growth in the faith.

Bloor Street United Church in midtown Toronto is an involved church, oftentimes courageous and sometimes willing to take risks. Its congregation is very experienced in relating the arts to worship and education. There is a long tradition of excellence in music, and it is nearly twenty years since the first liturgical dance, choreographed and danced by Susan Macpherson, took place in the chancel during an Advent service. Movie nights and excursions to plays and concerts involve many members in the continued enjoyment and discussion of the arts.

In the late seventies, an arts committee was formed at Bloor Street. Its purpose was to find ways of encouraging the arts, especially in connection with worship. The committee created experiences for the church, whereby the congregation would arrange a variety of art events and meet the artists. Everyone was delighted with the exhibitions of paintings in the church hall. One Remembrance Day Sunday, noted Canadian novelist Timothy Findley read from *The Wars* during the service. The Toronto Dance Theatre choreographed and presented a wonderful anti-nuclear war dance.

I was the first chair of the committee and Dr. Clifford Elliott, a minister of the church, was the clergy representative on the committee. He was very committed to the arts, both personally and in relation to ministry. One of the members of the committee, Dr. Johan Aitken, a long-time member of Bloor Street, told the rest of us about the work of sculptor Almuth Lutkenhaus and showed us a photograph of her sculpture *Crucified Woman*. We agreed we should go and see the sculpture in the artist's studio. We experienced it as compelling and honest. To us it portrayed strength, anguish, beauty, pain, and suffering. During our visit, the artist explained that she had not set out to create a religious sculpture. She had wanted to portray suffering and so had turned to the idea of the crucifixion. She used the female body, because, she said, "I am a woman."

All of the members of the committee were involved in the arts in some way, and we were unanimous in our agreement with Johan that we should bring the sculpture to the church. It was available only until the end of April, so the committee decided to exhibit the sculpture just before Palm Sunday. It would be in the church for about four weeks.

We agonized over where to put it. Several shows of paintings had been hung in the church hall, a large well-lighted room on the ground floor close to the nave, where a coffee hour was held each Sunday at the end of the worship service and church school. Each time there was a "show," the artist was invited to be present at a coffee hour. Such an event was announced ahead of time and everyone looked forward to meeting the artists and discussing, as well as viewing, their work. But this time the committee wanted the sculpture to be in the chancel at the front of the church. Wider discussion was needed before this could be done, so the sculpture was placed at one side of the nave and comments were invited. Although the judgement was not unanimously favourable, the sculpture was moved to the chancel during Holy Week to be there for Good Friday.

On Palm Sunday the sculpture was introduced to the congregation during the service, and people were asked to write comments in a book provided for that purpose. Reporters with microphones and television cameras also asked for comments. The city's largest newspaper carried in its Palm Sunday morning edition a front-page colour photo of Cliff and the sculpture. The headline read: "Nude Sculpture Greets Congregation." In contrast to the newspaper headline, the news report was thoughtful and went across the country.

The church immediately began to receive angry phone calls and letters expressing hurt and exasperation – even making threats. On the Tuesday evening after Easter, at the zone meeting of Presbytery, a long and lively discussion was held because Presbytery had received a letter complaining about the sculpture. A motion was made commending Dr. Elliott for having the sculpture in the church. Other letters of gratitude and appreciation were coming in. In both Hamilton and Montreal, hour-long radio phone-in programs took place. Newspapers in Hawaii, California, and Florida carried front-page stories.

The Good Friday service involved a neighbouring church and used as its theme the suffering of women. The offering was given to assist Battered Wives, an ecumenical agency. Confession and commitment to change were expressed by both women and men. Comments in the book were running eleven to one in favour of having the sculpture in the church. One comment said,

Splendid – yet demanding confession! As I meditate – I am confronted by the question – what part have I played in this crucifixion? Do not be afraid of publicity.

Another person said,

I'm very moved. Don't like all the feelings it arouses – but it certainly aroused some feelings. Thanks for taking the risk.

Some people acknowledged that it was all right to have the sculpture in the chancel on Good Friday but added, "Not on Easter Sunday. The empty cross, already in the chancel, is the symbol of Easter. . . . you're changing things around here."

On the Saturday before Easter, I went to talk to Cliff to see if he wanted the sculpture moved away from the chancel back to the side. The problem seemed to have changed from whether we should have the sculpture at all to whether it should be in the chancel. And it seemed to me that Cliff was the one with the most to lose in all of this. He was the one getting the calls and letters and threats. The committee made the decision, but he was the one who had to answer for it. He said:

This has been the most excruciating Holy Week in all of my ministry. But never has this congregation talked as much

about Christ and about suffering. I do want to go through with it. I feel as if I'm just beginning to see the world through the eyes of women.

On Easter Sunday, the *Crucified Woman* was still in the chancel, hanging just below the cross in front of the dossal curtain. The church was filled to capacity, and there was an air of expectancy as people shifted in the pews to make room for everyone to sit down. A few minutes into the service, Peggy Baker was dancing. Peggy, at that time a dancer with the company Dancemakers, had danced in services frequently, and this morning she was accompanied by a brass quintet playing "Crown him with many crowns." Margaret Zeidman, the soprano-soloist, sang "I know that my Redeemer liveth," and the congregation sang familiar Easter hymns and listened to one of the biblical accounts of the resurrection. There was more enthusiasm and energy than usual in the congregation, and Cliff seemed to have extra compassion, wisdom, honesty, humour, humility, and good news in this celebration of the Easter faith. As for the presence of the sculpture, congregation members observed that

Easter has a different feeling this year. For myself, the Crucified Woman *has provided me with the start of a valuable, searching experience. As I sit, listening to the excited voices of the members of my church, I am reminded of the voices long ago, determining the fate of Christ.*

৯ ৯ ৯

April 15, 1979, Easter Sunday at Bloor Street United Church. What a powerful and memorable service. The kind of service

that gives one renewed energy and faith. My eighteen-year-old nephew, who was a guest on Sunday, told me that the service had restored his faith, which had gradually been diluted. I was happy that the Crucified Woman *was in the church Easter Morning. I am happy to belong to a church that has faith in my ability to think for myself, that has the confidence to challenge my intellect and turn me around. The church was warm and alive that Sunday morning. And afterwards people flowed eagerly towards the chancel to view the sculpture. They felt involved. The atmosphere was electric, people were talking and communicating. It was so positive.*

Another person felt that the sculpture was in keeping with the rest of the service.

Images that will stay with me, and with others I have spoken to, for a long time: Peggy Baker dancing with the Crucified Woman *behind her; Margaret Zeidman singing Handel with the* Crucified Woman *behind her; Clifford Elliott speaking about darkness with the* Crucified Woman *behind him. Everything seemed to have a double impact. Emotional and thought-provoking.*

There were also people who were angry and hurt. Fewer of those were in the church. Many angry letters and phone calls were from people who had not seen the sculpture. A letter from a man in Sudbury who objected to the sculpture said he was writing "on behalf of forty women."

It is easy to say that the sculpture caused controversy. It is more accurate to say that it caused controversy to surface. But this very controversy indicated its timeliness. Thirty years ago, women remained mute and paralysed before the relentless onslaught of patriarchal theology. But those searching women were hurting, though no one much noticed. The sculpture was seen by some as an idea whose time had come and as a contribution to the universalizing of the Christ of faith.

Moving and appropriate statement on the suffering of humankind. We are long used to Black Christs as part of the universalizing of the gospel. Crucified Woman *is entirely within the same tradition.*

ᏒᏒ ᏒᏒ ᏒᏒ

The next thing you know, someone will give us a crucified Jew. Where will it ever end? This is an effective and needed statement of suffering womankind.

One way to describe the controversy is to say that the world broke in. Bloor Street, like many United churches, is used to being in charge of its own life and not used to having the world force its way in, in the form of intrusive television cameras, persistent journalists, and incessantly ringing telephones. There were members of the church who found all the publicity distinctly lacking in good taste.

Some people from the congregation had profound objections to the sculpture but were unable to give reasons for their thoughts and feelings. Others felt that the redemptive work of Christ was belittled by the sculpture.

A crucified woman is mocking the very basis of the Christian religion, the fact that Jesus Christ died on the cross and rose again. To take the ultimate sacrifice that Jesus made for the people of this world and turn it into a sculpture calculated to create controversy and get publicity is to me – blasphemous.

But all the questions caused Cliff Elliott to raise new ones.

What does the Incarnation mean? Who is on the cross today? Can we feel and share the hurt of women who have been oppressed and exploited? Can we see ourselves on the cross? In fact, this one piece of art has done more for deep soul searching than many, many words have been able to do.[1]

On the Easter Sunday, the sculptor, Almuth Lutkenhaus, was introduced to the congregation and was present at the coffee hour. Later, an evening meeting was scheduled for the congregation by the arts committee. A film showing Lutkenhaus at work was screened, and there was lively discussion. Here, and during the coffee hours, groups of two, three, four, or five people discussed theological issues raised by the sculpture: understandings of atonement, resurrection, Protestantism, "holy" space, the meaning of chancel, nave, narthex, transept, art, sculpture, crucifix, empty cross, idolatry, heresy, Christian feminism, suffering, redemption, Jesus of history, and the Christ of faith. Hundreds of people participated in such discussion so that the sculpture's potential for evoking theological discussion was clearly witnessed during those weeks.

The sculpture was returned to its owner at the end of April 1979. It was subsequently shown in both public and private galleries, but its permanent home was not found until 1986, at Emmanuel College.

Chapter Two

Celebration and Controversy: In the University

The sculpture was officially presented to Emmanuel College on May 10, 1986, at a Eucharistic celebration held outdoors. Dr. C. Douglas Jay, principal of the college, received the gift of the sculpture from the artist, Almuth Lutkenhaus. Ms. Lutkenhaus had very limited energy due to a debilitating disease, but she spoke eloquently of the journey of the sculpture from an Ontario school classroom, where she had been artist-in-residence, to this place.

Bright sunlight, a cloudless sky, and over a hundred invited guests contributed to a feeling of celebration and joy. The site that had been chosen for the sculpture was the lower level of a terraced area with a half-circle stone retaining wall about forty feet from the sculpture. This area was first used that day and has become, since that time, a "natural" gathering space for worship.

Alexandra Caverly-Lowery, from the faculty of dance at York University, and a graduate in theology, choreographed "Our Lullabies Rebirthed," a dance based on Isaiah 66:7-13 and Galatians 3:26-28. Three dancers, in long gowns of deep dark colours heightened and shadowed by the sunlight, used their female bodies to tell a story of the suffering and the celebration of women. Music for the dance was composed by Maggie Burston and played by the Ardeleana Trio. Alexandra wrote the script of the dance in poetic form.

> – *I said to my soul*
> *Be still!*
> *And let dark come upon you* –
> *Darkness of God, My God* – *Why have you forsaken me?*
> *Weeping as a woman weeps* – *as if the earth were bleeding* –
> *Weary with my moaning* – *My soul poured out* – *like water* –
> *Bones* – *all out of joint!*
> *My heart like wax* – *melted in my breast* –
> *Milk mingled with the blood* – *dried up now* –
> *Dust of Death.*
> *No voice to sing sweet lullabies* – *just woman* – *wrapped in silence*
> *Rocking in her grief* –
> *Torn out the sobs!*
> *No lullabies.*
> *The children of our pain* – *WHERE ARE THEY?* – *earth cries out*
> *with voice to tell the stories* –
> *My brothers' and my sisters' blood yet calling from the ground.*
> *And Lord have mercy* – *far too softly spoke*
> *must SCREAM across the silence and the space* –
> *It is enough! and It is finished!*
> *Split wineskin* – *old and festered wounds of the world* –
>
> *Veil Rent! My God* – *My heart of soul is torn in two*
> *And You must lay therein* – *within the wounds* –

open now — the noonday sun pours across the space —
without — within —
to reach and touch and love all that
Love has birthed — bursting Life and lusty cries
across the earth where all
remember —
Tears and Dreams and Laughter now
Flow mingled down —
Our common pain, our common joy — our lullabies rebirthed.
And children walk the land
Where all have circled on the common Holy ground
And every voice is heard.

The litany of thanksgiving used at the liturgy on the day of the presentation conveys the nuances of thoughts and feelings that day, a way of telling the story of the *Crucified Woman* and a way of doing theology.

One: God is the giver of gifts of great worth, birthed from
      pain and love.
All: We rejoice and give thanks for these gifts, O God.
One: Some are given the gift to write music, speak, dance or
      lead; some to encourage, comfort, persist; each witness
      to God's promise of life made new.
All: We rejoice and give thanks for these gifts, O God.
One: This day we especially give thanks for the insight,
      creativity, skill and generosity of Almuth Lutkenhaus;
      and for the Crucified Woman, *which calls some to*
      repentance; some to healing and wholeness; and which
      startles our vision of Christ's image in all.
All: We rejoice and give thanks for this gift, O God.

The presentation hymn, written by Sylvia Dunstan, sets forth a theology that is unusually inclusive and at the same time quite traditional. One of the problems with many services of worship is that we do not really listen to what we sing, because the words of the hymns are too familiar. How can the same salvation story sound new? Hymns that are familiar are the ones that many of us long to sing but we often do not notice what the words say. Much of our theology is learned through hymns. This one is called "Re-membering" and is sung to the tune Ebenezer.

We remember, Risen Jesus,
We remember at the tomb
that the women stood there staring
Awestruck at the opened womb.
They ran back to tell the story
"He is risen; Do not fear!"
But the rest were unbelieving
at a truth they could not hear.

We remember, Risen Jesus
We remember how you said
that a child of God once slaughtered
One day would rise from the dead.
These are words for all your people
All have promise of new birth.
So we rise to seek your promise,
coming forth to claim our worth.

The last line of the hymn is remarkably close to the personal testimony of a woman who said, "When I saw the sculpture in Bloor Street United on Easter morning, 1979, I had a resurrection of my female worth that changed my life."

After the service we had lunch, a garden party. The preparation and presentation of food, traditionally connected to women's identity, can be an ambiguous symbol for women. The catered meal was an attempt to eat together without exploiting anyone.

The presentation and liturgy on May 10 at noon was the culmination of a Friday and Saturday celebration of women's gifts at Emmanuel College called "Womanly Arts." On the Friday evening, there was a cabaret of songs, dance, music, stories, and poetry reading in the midst of a display of women's textile arts, quilts, embroidery, paintings and weaving. On Saturday morning there was a variety of workshops on music, art, health care, politics, and body movement. Women talked to each other about all the things they like to tell each other if left on their own.

In June 1988, an international conference, "Women in Inter-Faith Dialogue," was held at Emmanuel College. Toronto was chosen by the World Council of Churches as a city that already had a lively inter-faith dialogue. Women came from Africa, Asia, Europe, the Middle East, Latin America, the Caribbean, and all over North America for the first global conference of women in inter-faith dialogue.

Throughout the twilight hours of that Friday evening, much like the "Womanly Arts" Friday evening in 1986, sixty women were praying, eating, singing, and dancing. That may not sound remarkable but this was a Jewish Sabbath supper and the women were Buddhist, Hindu, Sikh, Baha'i, Islamic, Native North American, Wicca (Goddess), Christian, and Jewish. The young rabbi, taking leadership with only women present, told us that this was the first time that she had officiated knowing that *everyone* wanted her to do well!

Each day of the inter-faith conference, there was an opportunity to be a participant-observer in ritual acts as varied as Hindu puja, Muslim prayer, Buddhist meditation, Wiccan incantation, Christian worship, and a Jewish Sabbath meal. Eating was important at the dialogue. Many religions have dietary regulations at their centre, and it is traditionally women who preside over the preparation and serving of food in their homes. Several of the meals, all of them vegetarian and catered, were eaten in the college garden near the *Crucified Woman*. Some of the rituals took place there, as well as conversations, whether perfunctory or passionate. The sculpture was often the topic of discussion. Women from other faith traditions seemed to understand the sculpture and to know that it connected the suffering of women with a central Christian motif – the crucifixion of Jesus. The farewell ritual for the conference took place around the sculpture. With hands joined in a circle, the woman moved in dance forms around the sculpture. The sculpture itself has sometimes been interpreted as a woman conveying suffering in the language of dance.

As I have emphasized, there was a great sense of nurturing and joy on the occasion of the presentation, and at other times, such as the conference, but there were three years of contentious discussion at Emmanuel College before that day. The artist offered the sculpture as a gift to the college in 1983. Much time was spent in dealing with the various committees involved in the decision-making process and in countering the opposition of several professors and students who objected strongly to the college accepting the gift.

One of the committees that spent a lot of time considering the appropriateness of the gift as a work of art, and who also dealt with the question of where to put it, was the Victoria University Senate Art Committee. Emmanuel College

(Theology) and Victoria College (Arts) together constitute Victoria University, and although each college has its own budget, curriculum, faculty, and building, property is owned by Victoria University and decisions about art acquisitions are made by the Senate Art Committee.

At the end of 1983, the Senate Art Committee provided the Senate with slide illustrations of possible locations for the sculpture. Rather than basing the decision on the slides, however, the Senate decided that it should view the work itself.

Consequently, the sculpture was brought and placed in the Birge-Carnegie reading room for viewing. Members of the committee, as well as others, found the viewing useful and the cause of readjusted assumptions. Although not all the members of the committee looked favourably on the sculpture, it reported to the Senate in October 1984 that the work was of sufficient aesthetic merit to be accepted by Victoria University. The Report of the Senate Art Committee of October 5, 1984, submitted by its chair David Blostein, a professor in the English Department, provided the committee's rationale as well as its recommendation.

> *The Senate Art Committee's task was to decide whether the work was of sufficient aesthetic merit to be accepted by Victoria University. We find a basic ambiguity in that injunction, for while as a matter of legality, a gift to a part of Victoria University can be accepted only by the university as a whole, the aesthetic status of, say, a painting of flowers might be quite inadequate if it were offered to the Emmanuel Chapel but quite splendid if it were offered to Annesley Hall. Nevertheless, at the May 9 meeting of the Senate, the Committee was directed to concentrate on the context of*

Victoria University; but we still hope the Senate will not find us perverse in finding it difficult to forget that Ms. Lutkenhaus's gift was specifically offered to Emmanuel College.

Aesthetic merit is not an absolute. Social, political, ethical or religious connotations may all have proper place in aesthetic judgement, and certainly it is unlikely that the associations of a figure in cruciform could honestly be detached from 2,000 years of cultural heritage.

But should it be regarded from the point of representational tradition? What if, for instance, the distorted face, which is devoid of any discernible personality beneath its generalized sorrow, is, like a work of Barlach or Kollwicz, indicative of the final effect of the particular kinds of suffering that women have undergone? What if the contrast between sexy torso and unsexed, unpersoned face indicates a connection between the two facts? What if the discrepancy between the pert adolescent breasts and the functionally swollen nipples is a reminder of a false aesthetic ideal of womanly beauty? What if the cross-hatched grooves that emphasize and in places exaggerate the contours of this body remind one of the scourging of Christ's flesh? What is the voluntary act suggested by the turned right hand? Why are the pudenda uncovered? Why should they not be? Is there beauty in a woman's suffering contemplated? Is there beauty in a Christ's suffering contemplated? Were women literally crucified in Roman times? To what extent is the suffering of one of the hundreds of thousands of anonymous persons who died on the cross worthy of aesthetic contemplation? Of religious meditation? Of theological argumentation?

The members of the Senate Art Committee have separately and together, come to a conclusion ... that the value of the "Crucified Woman" – its aesthetic value – seems to increase the closer its context is to a religious one. And so even those members who would object fairly strenuously to its location anywhere else on the Victoria University Campus, find the donor's proposed setting, Emmanuel College, to be appropriate. The Senate Art Committee therefore finds the "Crucified Woman" aesthetically acceptable for location at Emmanuel College, if the college so desires.

The Senate Art Committee also made reference to a study carried out by Professor E.A. Trott in her aesthetics class. Professor Trott asked the members of the class to view the sculpture and write down their responses and reactions. The class later discussed the following two questions: Is it a work of art? What contributions would you want to make to the college deliberations concerning its suitability for display and hence its acceptability as a gift?

One student said:

Her face is of most interest, for in many respects it contrasts with her body. Like the image of Christ upon the cross, the woman's face is bent forward slightly and has fallen to one side. This particular side of her face has her features distorted (melted down). Expression is one of pain (almost despairing). Her hair is limp and crowns her face in the manner of the traditional presentations of Christ upon the cross.

Another student noted that "there are no holes in the palms of her hands or her feet."

One response had poetic form:

female crucifix
what have they done – victimized
depressing
distress – distortion
face, hanging hair
what is society doing to you, woman
calls for something to be done

what is the purpose of the sacrifice
is this hope of resurrection
what is resurrection
new understanding of values, new relationships

it provokes thoughts of what can be done to relieve
the situation
woman misunderstood – abused – victimized

pity (look up Aristotle)

maybe someone understands ... requires colossal forgiveness
crucifixion of grace – everything woman stands for
youth – development and place disallowed
disrespect for inability to conceive of grace
no room for grace in today's world
repudiation of grace, the effects of grace

today – aggression – oppression
pride of power (anti-Christian)

no time for grace

*vulnerability of womanhood, grace
need for restraint.*

Several comments made reference to inconsistent modes of presentation within the aesthetic form, as well as deviation from representation norms:

... the contrast of a distorted face with a well-formed youthful body;

ॐ ॐ ॐ

... from a representational view (art as symbol), were one to view it as a Christ-like portrayal text, the position of the hands, the nakedness, the absence of the cross, the absence of nail marks, all stand as signs that depart from traditional symbolic art forms of the crucifixion;

ॐ ॐ ॐ

... the "sorrowful" countenance (traditionally Christ's face does not portray sorrow, grief, or despair but rather resignation and peace.)

Students saw the sculpture's potential for stimulating thought as highly desirable within a university setting.

The historical status of Victoria and Emmanuel as religiously federated colleges would be complemented by displaying the sculpture without committing the colleges to restrictive dogma, and the adaptation and intellectual flexibility in responding to ongoing social and human concerns would be articulated in the acceptance and display of this thought-provoking piece.

The students in the aesthetics class and the members of the Senate Art Committee independently came to the conclusion that there were more reasons for accepting than declining the sculpture. There was still a great deal of discussion at the Senate itself. More members were present than is usually the case and the meeting lasted longer. The Senate agreed to accept the gift "if Emmanuel so desires" and thus began a period of many discussions among Emmanuel College faculty, students, and Council. Private money was offered to bronze the sculpture so that an outdoor setting would be possible. An alumna of Victoria University said,

I find the decision that they would object to the sculpture anywhere else on the campus very strange – but then I guess most of the works of art they do have are very safe – Group of Seven and male professors in black robes. Although I think there is a portrait of Wesley's mother. I wonder what her life was really like as opposed to what shows in that picture.

The location became an integral part of the decision, so the location was decided first and then the decision was also made to accept the gift and proceed with the installation. The installation design was by Alexander Czumaczenka and the installation itself was carried out by Stephenson Construction.

Victoria University gardener Peter Hooiveld liked the sculpture very much and prepared for its installation by removing a dying tree and having three new silver birches planted, one at each side and one behind the sculpture. Junipers and colourful flowering annuals were planted around the sculpture. It became the gardener's favourite garden. When he retired, his co-workers presented him with a painting of the sculpture garden. The security staff liked the *Crucified Woman* and also knew the tendencies of male university students: the sculpture was well-lighted, but security came regularly at party-times! When the sculpture was in place several days before the official presentation, I was anxious lest there be any vandalism. Both the gardener and the security staff "protected" her and comforted me. Five years later there has still been no vandalism, although a Toronto newspaper responded to a phone call and carried a photo of the sculpture with Christmas lights on it. Later one of the male students who had done this expressed remorse.

There was a clear gender distinction among those who wanted it and those who did not, but there were many men who participated visibly and continuously in the controversy on the side of having the sculpture. Ted Reeve, a doctoral student, saw the arrival of the sculpture and wrote this about his feelings:

The woman of both scorn and praise had arrived as a member of the Emmanuel community. It was a sunny spring day when she first appeared; yet clouds threatened, as did her appearance strike dark thoughts into the minds of some.

Naked, beautiful, but positioned in agony, she stood for all to see.

The workmen erecting her pedestal did so with expertise and care. A large crane lowered her between the scaffold. A workman on either side held her hand gently and guided her into her resting place. Her feet bound with tape to avoid the splash of concrete, the workman began to pour the liquid rock that would secure her for posterity.

Observing the drama, I watched people come to stare; some in disbelief; some with embarrassed smiles; many who congregated in small groups laughed openly as if to taunt, to shout "come down off of there if you're so great."

Christ-like indeed! A passionate display of love for the world. Vulnerable, yet with a heaven-bound stare that transcends her agonized pose and the jeering crowd below.

One of the professors at Victoria said he would not be able to walk by it. Another wanted it placed where he could not see it from his window. Many did not care one way or another but opined that those that did not like it did not have to look at it. One professor said he was sexually aroused – it was "too erotic." As I write this, someone today has placed purple flowers and tulle around the base of the sculpture.

Students who were at the college in the years of the controversy remember the energy and joy. There was a great deal of argument but little malice. Theologians respect each other even though they may differ. One of the students who had graduated in 1984 wrote from Nipigon in May 1986:

Thanks for the notice re: Womanly Arts. I sang a hearty hallelujah and did a quick fandango when I realized that the Crucified Woman is finally coming to Emmanuel. Although I'm not able to be there for the celebration, my heart will be with all of you as you dance with every muscle in your hearts on this important occasion.

At the Emmanuel College graduation ceremonies in 1990, Robert Dalgleish, the student valedictorian, said,

How could we have appreciated what we might learn from a scared and suffering, yet hauntingly beautiful young woman, who stands mutely in the courtyard, flowers wilting at her feet, a silent memorial?

Chapter Three

Artistic and Theological Differences: A Transforming Story

The sculpture is a bronzed, elongated female figure in cruciform, naked with outstretched arms. The seven-foot figure is placed securely on a four-foot concrete base. There is no cross. The feet point downward, the breasts are taut, and the head drops to one side. There is beauty in the naked female body of the sculpture; there is pain and suffering in the face. The position of the hands, the nakedness, the absence of the cross, the absence of nail marks, the female, rather than male, body are departures from traditional norms of representations of the crucifixion.

These artistic differences seem to involve viewers theologically. Some of the theology that emerges is not unlike traditional ways of speaking of the faith. Feminist theology is not necessarily at odds with fidelity to the creeds. But there are theological differences, as well as artistic. Theological imagination seems to develop in the context of the *Crucified Woman*, and this may be because of the differences. In the biblical records, especially the gospel accounts of the life of Jesus, it is primarily by the study of the differences in the stories that theology has flourished.

As a Christian education event and as an occasion for theological discussion, the sculpture is profoundly significant. The story can be told, in part, by quotations from people who have seen the sculpture. An eighty-five-year-old woman said, "I'm glad I lived to see this day. I think it's wonderful." An eleven-year-old girl said, "I like it. It makes the church a lot better."

Women saw themselves in the *Crucified Woman*, and spoke of the impact of the sculpture on their self-understanding and their faith, as well as their experience as participants in a male-centred church. If the responses seem repetitive, it is because, in many cases, feelings were similar. In the early days of the contemporary women's movement, women were surprised and comforted when the stories of other women's lives were like their own. A sense of community replaced the loneliness and isolation that many women experienced.

The usual image of a man hung on a tree really imprisoned me to the idea of a male God. The image of a woman liberates me into the idea that my being a woman allows me to identify with God's act. Beautiful, powerful, a challenge to take up the cross and not be a passive bystander.

❧ ❧ ❧

To begin with, I was not convinced by the pictures that it would be a good thing to have the sculpture in the church, but after seeing it, it makes the crucifixion, which was quite distant to me, a much closer, more meaningful reality. I don't go to church myself, and I certainly do not feel encouraged to do so when I see the reaction of "good" Christians and members of their churches who speak out against something like the Crucified Woman *only because they prefer their traditional, undisturbed ways to the most disturbing and always contemporary demand of Christ. The crucifixion of Christ is not an event of the past but is carried on in many ways today whenever a human being created in the image of God and invited to be reborn in Christ suffers injustice, torture, and death, many in an even more cruel way than Jesus Christ.*

❧ ❧ ❧

The Crucified Woman *left me in awe. In spite of thirty odd years of attending church, I cannot remember an impact like "she" made on me in the name of Christ. It is really something to see one of one's own kind up there, and to know, so specifically, that Jesus Christ died and rose and lives for me, a woman, a sinner, and somehow once again, a believer, rededicated to Christ.*

❧ ❧ ❧

A very moving sculpture that allows me to identify more closely with the crucifixion and elevates, at last, woman to the ultimate suffering. An important experience and a peaceful one.

❧ ❧ ❧

I find it important that women can see a depiction of their suffering which tells them they are not alone and that, even though they have suffered like many other women, they have survived and what is more important, their ability to love has survived – they, their children, and the world need this.

ta ta ta

When I first saw Almuth Lutkenhaus' Crucified Woman, *my heart journeyed among the spiritually beautiful women I had known. I recalled the radiant faces of women around the world, all lined up with pleasure, purpose, and pain. Together they became a glorious company of Christ-like women. There was hope mixed with anguish as I named them "Christ-like."*

ta ta ta

A memorable sight. Compassion and suffering united in a figure. Woman as the ground of being. God made woman as symbol of incarnate creative power – or love.

ta ta ta

The sculpture honours women and their gift of love, which has been abused. There are so many abused women in our society and so many abused by those they trust and love – and women go on giving that love only to be hit, slapped, kicked, punched, abused in every way. And yet I can't remember any other work of art showing women as love abused, betrayed, and abandoned.

ta ta ta

A fine piece of sculpture. It is good to see a woman as representative of crucified humanity and as a symbol of the crucified Christ.

Some theologians would object to these comments and for theological reasons. They make the point that while the oppression and pain and suffering of women may be identified *with* crucifixion, the particular suffering that women experience because of their gender ought not to be identified *as* crucifixion. The central point in this objection is that women suffer as victims, and Jesus is not a victim. In fact, Jesus *chose* to go to the cross. The garden of Gethsemane story is interpreted by these theologians as Jesus' choice to go through with something that could have been avoided; Jesus was acting in obedience to God.

The garden of Gethsemane story appears in Matthew, Mark, and Luke, the synoptic Gospels. In John, there is a different account of the period of time just before the betrayal. As the gospel accounts illustrate by their differences, there are varied details, emphases and interpretations. In the synoptic account, there is a narrative quality that draws the reader into the interesting details and dialogue. But an overly literal hearing of the details of Holy Week is hazardous. Behind the years of classical theology, the only biblical words attributed to Jesus that would support a theory of his choosing to go to the cross in obedience to God are "remove this cup, nevertheless not my will but thine be done." All of the accounts indicate that at the time Jesus spoke these words, the disciples were asleep and the prayer containing these words took place a stone's throw from where they were sleeping. So I do not think it is helpful to insist on a literal theological interpretation.

Instead of taking this account literally we might ask what the gospel writers were telling us about God. Perhaps they were struggling with how God can be all-loving and, at the same time, all-powerful. Or perhaps the writer was intent on showing us how human Jesus was. Many human beings can identify with this prayer; soldiers have often seen their suffering and the likelihood of their death as the carrying out of God's will. Many women have seen their faithfulness unto death to an abusive partner in marriage as the carrying out of God's will. Surely the Abraham and Isaac story tells us that God does not *need* human suffering and sacrifice. God is not victimizer. But I think it is too much to say that Jesus was not a victim in any way. To be betrayed and abandoned is surely to be a victim. Betrayal and abandonment are ways of suffering that many women experience.

I do not think that Jesus chose to suffer, but rather that Jesus chose to love. Women also choose to love. All who choose to love enter into conflict with those who fear love. Suffering is not itself the choice but the consequence of the choice to love. As a symbol that connects women's suffering and the crucifixion, the sculpture both is and is not "complete." To be helpful as a work of art, every aspect does not have to fit precisely within the traditional theological interpretation of the biblical record. In fact, as I have already said, I believe the differences are especially important. The Bible itself is not internally consistent and does not ask us to be. But for many people, a biblical image or symbol suddenly came alive for them in response to the sculpture. Both men and women saw the abuse of women as a betrayal of women's gift of love. Betrayal and abandonment are dimensions of the crucifixion story and are the experiences of many women, both personally and collectively. The betrayal and abandonment of Jesus by those who were intimate friends, the continuing betrayal and abandonment of Christ by all of us, are aspects of the crucifixion that are clearly seen in the sculpture.

In her book *Suffering,* German theologian Dorothee Soelle says,

> *It is impossible to distinguish Jesus' suffering from that of other people as though Jesus alone awaited God's help. The scream of suffering contains all the despair of which a person is capable, and in this sense every scream is a scream for God. All extreme suffering evokes the experience of being forsaken by God. In the depth of suffering, people see themselves as abandoned and forsaken by everyone.*[2]

The Christian hope is that betrayal and abandonment do not have to go on and on.

In addition to the important themes of betrayal and abandonment, women identified with the theme of resurrection. In the way in which we understand that God acted for good in the chaos of the crucifixion, some women were able to see grace and hope in their own suffering bodies. One woman, who chose to be anonymous, wrote this reflection on her own healing:

By His Wounds You Have Been Healed

O God,
through the image of a woman
crucified on the cross
I understand at last.

For over half of my life
I have been ashamed
of the scars I bear.
These scars tell an ugly story,
a common story,

about a girl who is the victim
when a man acts out his fantasies.

In the warmth, peace and sunlight of your presence
I was able to uncurl the tightly clenched fists.
For the first time
I felt your suffering presence with me
in that event.
I have known you as a vulnerable baby,
as a brother, as a father.
Now I know you as a woman.
You were there with me
as the violated girl
caught in helpless suffering.

The chains of shame and fear
no longer bind my heart and body.
A slow fire of compassion and forgiveness
is kindled.
My tears fall now
for man as well as woman.

You, God,
can make our violated bodies
vessels of love and comfort
to such a desperate man.
I am honoured
to carry this womanly power
within my body and soul.

You were not ashamed of your wounds
You showed them to Thomas

as marks of your ordeal and death.
I will no longer hide these wounds of mine.
I will bear them gracefully,
They tell a resurrection story.
(1 Peter 2:24)

Art is not intended as a literal representation of something else. Children, perhaps because they are closer to seeing things for the "first" time, are able to make authentic responses to what an artist has done, rather than what is not done. One child said,

Anybody knows that's not Jesus. But looking at it makes you think about Jesus. Everybody's thinking about Jesus. You can tell they are because they're all talking about Jesus.

Another child said,

You know they sometimes say Jesus is the Lamb of God, and they don't really mean that Jesus is a lamb. I don't know what they really do mean, but I guess they liked lambs.

Many people do find the biblical metaphor of Jesus as Lamb of God to be helpful. But it is also confusing. It is preposterous to think of a lamb as willing sacrifice, of choosing to suffer. Lambs do not usually turn into shepherds, but both metaphors are used for Jesus and some people find them helpful and healing. That is the experience of many people with the sculpture *Crucified Woman*: helpful, healing, transforming. The artistic and theological differences provide energy and imagination for new interpretations that are always emerging. It is important to find suitable ways to talk about

God in our present context that have meaning for our time.

Traditional disciplinary norms of theology have required that theologians deal with the intellectual problems posed by philosophy and history and the sciences and advance the cause of theology in the context of the dominant culture. But there are also ways of doing theology that say no to "positions" of tradition and authority, and more people are taking part in the ongoing creation of new theologies.

As one of the contemporary expressions of theology, women's theology draws on the populist, community-based characteristic of liberation theology and on the personal struggle usually associated with existential theology. Liberation theologies begin from the perspective of those not normally included, the oppressed and the powerless, and interpret the Bible and the faith out of their living community. Existential theology begins with the questions of the self. The qualities of longing, commitment, urgency, and anguish found in prayer are existential. There is much passion in existential theology, but there is not less intellect, and certainly feelings and ideas do not have to be separated. Women's theology, as it asks new questions, does so with the passion of liberal struggle for personal freedom combined with the solidarity of community, the populist perspective of the oppressed. By its urgent and personal quality, although it may be only one person's work, women's theology engages the "other," whether listener or reader, because personally pressing dilemmas are also important to other people. A living and inclusive church is willing to pay attention in order to hear the many ways in which sensitive and thoughtful people, many of whom are women, speak of their faith.

Almuth Lutkenhaus has frequently been asked about the sculpture *Crucified Woman*. She has always said that she wanted to portray human suffering, and since she was a woman, she chose a female body. She told the group attending the installation of the sculpture at Emmanuel College in May 1986 that she had been deeply moved by the many women who had told her that, for the first time, they felt close to Christ when they saw her sculpture. Like many artists, Lutkenhaus sees herself as an instrument for an archetypal and external message. Straightforward about the way artists work, she says, "They just work, and they may think about meanings afterward."

Ways of knowing in theology and ways of knowing in art are very similar. Both require the participation of the community. The sculpture provided the opportunity for many people to find the words for the saving story. To do theology means to listen, as well as to talk and write. The willing participation of so many people in responding to the sculpture depended on the nature of artistic expression. Religious art carries with it a particular norm. Its value is not only aesthetic; rather it has value through its relationship with a community and the meaning that it evokes within that community.

Works of art evoke creative response: conflict, ambiguity, and anguish are expressed in the responses of the people because they are expressed in the sculpture. The creative imagination knows that change comes in the context of conflict. Artists trust their own insight and are unwilling to submit to rigid control; but they are also able and willing to recognize and respect differences. To be understood is more important than to be agreed with – in both theology and art. In telling this story, and in using the responses of many people, there is an affirmation of art as a way of doing theology.

Chapter Four

Protestantism and Art: A Conflicted Relationship

Art is, in some ways, a reflection of the world that we live in, but it is more than a reflection: it is what we truly look like. Theologians have sometimes said that art is a prophetic reflection and, as such, an agent that compels creative change. Others simply say that art makes you stop and think, then act in a different way. Art is often connected, even identified, with the compelling power of beauty, but art does not have to be beautiful to call us to who we are.

Theologian Paul Tillich says that Protestantism requires us to look "at the human situation in its depths of estrangement and despair." Artists see and care who we are and enable us to defend ourselves against destruction, or at least to warn us. Benjamin Britten's *War Requiem* uses the traditional Latin requiem text interspersed with various poems of the English soldier-poet Wilfred Owen. The title page says: "My subject is war and the pity of war. The poetry is in the pity. All a poet can do today is warn."

Sometimes art is thought to be a frill, entertainment, something to do in the time that is left over, and essentially inconsequential. But Picasso said that art is an instrument of war to defend ourselves against the forces of darkness and brutality. He was painting in the context of war. One of his most important paintings is *Guernica*. Guernica, a small town in the Basque region, was destroyed in the first experience of what came to be called saturation bombing. Picasso painted this horror, fragments of human beings, fragments of animals, fragments of houses, and Paul Tillich said that this painting was "the symbol of the cross." Tillich said, "*Guernica* shows the human situation without any cover," and named it "the best present-day Protestant religious painting."[3] We may see something already seen as if for the first time, when we see it painted or meet it in poetry.

Artists warn us by their own sensitivity. During the First World War, white rabbits were taken down into submarines, because they reacted to a lack of oxygen before human beings did. So when the white rabbits died, the submarine had to come up for air. Artists are like those white rabbits. They warn us of how close we are to dying, and in so doing, they enable us to go on living. Dying for us so that we may live, artists tell us about God.

A powerful and ambiguous story that comes to us out of the horror of the Holocaust tells of a group of prisoners about to enter the gas chambers. Somehow the commanding SS officer learned that one of the women prisoners had been a dancer, and he ordered her to dance for him. She did, and as she danced, she seized his gun and shot him. She was immediately put to death, as she must have known she would be.

Did dancing make this woman once again a unique person? Did dancing transform her from a depersonalized prisoner, a number, into a dancer, the embodiment of a free spirit? She risked her life in her own way. Not able to live, she chose how she would die. She danced to her own death. In making her last choice, she embodied spirited choice. Did she die, not merely because of us, but for us, like another Jew, the one Christians named Christ?

Creativity, as well as art, is always a gift. When we think of art and artists, we think of both freedom and discipline, but there are other dimensions of power to consider. What art do we get to see? What art do we not get to see? How much are artistic criteria determined by the dominant voices in any culture? Classical artists are men, but stories are coming to light such as that of Camille Claudel, Rodin's student and lover, an artist who actually sculpted many works for which Rodin took credit.[4]

There are open questions as to who decides what is "good" art, as well as which ones of the many creative human endeavours shall be called art. Knitting, making quilts, cooking, creative activities usually undertaken by women, are undervalued and rarely thought of as art.

The Danish writer Isak Dinesen, whose life in Africa came to widespread public attention through the popular film *Out of Africa*, wrote a short story called *Babette's Feast*, which was also made into a film.[5] In this story, there is transforming power in the art of preparing and serving food. Babette is an older woman, big and dark, who shares nothing of her past. She came to Jutland as a fugitive from strife-torn France to keep house for two sisters. Their father, founder and minister of a tiny, austere Christian sect, had died, and both of his beautiful and self-denying daughters, their fair hair now grey, honoured his memory by their devotion to good works in caring for members of the community. They brought food and visited the sick and elderly. One of the sisters, particularly gifted in music, gave up a potential professional career as a singer, understanding her sacrifice to be God's will. Certainly it was her father's!

The lives of the people in that community mirrored the landscape: unyielding, unfrivolous, unforgiving. Wind, rain, sea, and sky were relentless reminders of the harsh loneliness of their relationship to God and to each other. In lives of hardship, obedience, and austerity, they took themselves very seriously.

At first, members of the community looked askance at a foreign woman in their midst, but soon they recognized the transforming power in Babette's work. Dinesen says,

> *In the course of time not a few of the brotherhood included Babette's name in their prayers, and thanked God for the speechless stranger, the dark Martha in the house of their two fair Marys. The stone which the builders had almost refused had become the headstone of the corner.*[6]

Babette came into the community in a rainstorm, wrapped in a cape and shrouded in mystery. She bargained at the market and cooked the food that was available on the sisters' frugal budget. As the time came for the celebration of the 100th birthday of the sisters' deceased father, Babette asked if she could buy the food and prepare the meal in her own way. She had unexpectedly received some money from France. The sisters agreed, expecting that she would leave their employ and return to France. Babette imported French wines, crystal, china, fresh fruit, quail, and other exotic foods. She prepared the food and served it in delicious sauces, piquant and sweet.

One of the guests was a general who, in his bright uniform covered with decorations, shone like "a golden pheasant or a peacock, in this sedate party of black crows and jackdaws."[7] As

Babette served each new dish and wine, the general was reminded of another dinner given in his honour at the finest restaurant in Paris. He recognized the food as having been created by the Parisian chef known throughout France as the culinary genius of the age. What had made it all most unheard of was that the chef was a woman.

All around the general, those austere, resistant, life-denying human beings began to melt – perhaps to a place that they had longed for. In the glow of the candles, the joy of the wine, and the goodness of the food, their faces softened, their bodies relaxed, and they smiled! There were twelve of them around the table, and it was a Eucharist. Grace came to them through Babette's feast. Knowing that they were blessed, they could reach out to each other in forgiveness and laughter. Outside, after the feast, the air was still cold, but the stars seemed closer and the people laughed. The community was transformed. Next morning, the sisters thanked Babette and asked her when she would be leaving for France. Babette told them that she could not afford to return, as the feast had taken all of her money. One of the sisters put her arms around Babette and whispered, "I feel, Babette, that this is not the end. In Paradise, you will be the great artist that God meant you to be. . . . how you will enchant the angels."[8]

Protestantism and art have had a conflicted relationship. Catholicism has affirmed symbol and sacrament while Protestantism has emphasized word. During the time of the Protestant Reformation, much Christian art was destroyed. Calvinists emptied their churches of all pictures, statues, and symbols, because for them the void was the most powerful symbol of God's presence. In several strands of Christianity, as well as in other world religions, there is concern that visual symbols, rather than pointing beyond themselves to God (an assumption in Catholic thought), will simply attract attention and become idols, taking the place of God. But neither theologians, philosophers, nor any of the rest of us want to destroy something that we love, and for Martin Luther, one of the great Protestant reformers and writers, music was a passion. Luther wrote in defence of the arts:

> *I am not of the opinion, as are the heterodox, that for the sake of the Gospel, all arts should be rejected and eliminated; rather, I feel strongly that all the arts, and particularly music, should be placed in the service of Him, who has created and given them.*[9]

Christine on the Cross, a two-foot sculpture, appeared in St. James Chapel at Union Theological Seminary in New York in 1984. Professor Phyllis Trible was quoted by Bobbie Crawford in the article "A Female Crucifix," as saying, "Through familiarity, traditional representation of the cross may dull awareness of its multiple dimensions."[10] And *Christine on the Cross* is no traditional representation. There is a cross with a lowered crossbar on which her legs are spread and nailed. Her arms are pulled upward and nailed above her head to the vertical bar. The sculptor, James M. Murphy, said that he had tried to sculpt a crucifixion.

> *Last Easter my sketch in soft clay took the shape of a woman. I realized thereby that the world's rejection and hatred of women culminates in crucifying the female Christ.*[11]

In 1984, another "crucified woman" sculpture appeared. *Christa*, a nude female figure with outstretched arms on a cross, sculpted by artist Edwina Sandys, was shown in New

York's Episcopal Cathedral of St. John the Divine. Dean James Parks Morton said that the sculpture forced people to think theologically and to realize how bound they were to stereotypes and to literalness. Morton also reminded contemporary Christians of the mystic Julian of Norwich, who in the fourteenth century,

> speaks of Christ as our mother, and the blessed sacrament coming from the breasts of Christ. Astonishing language. One is dealing with metaphor, with art. And deep theology, like deep poetry, is not literal stuff.[12]

Carter Heyward, a contemporary American theologian, notes that some Christian feminists are concerned that *Christa* could seem to glorify suffering. Heyward suggests instead that *Christa* connects with "relational nuances" in the life of Jesus.

> When we are most genuinely in touch with one another and most respectful of our differences, we most fully embody Christa. As members of her sacred body, we give and receive power to bless, to touch, and to heal one another, we who are lovers and friends, sisters and brothers, of all creatures and of the earth, our common home.[13]

Artistic ways of knowing are precise, but metaphorical rather than literal. Poets use words with such exquisite precision that we want to memorize the words; they shadow us. We can not "say it in our own words," because we do not want to lose the power and perfection of poetic words. The Bible does that too: "the very hairs of your head are numbered" or "the heavens opened." It is in the nature of artistic expression that it not be literal, and so it is impossible to deal directly with the question asked by some people about the sculpture: "Is this meant to be Christ?" The only answer is "yes and no."

A widely read Canadian author, the late Margaret Laurence, dealt with this question and offered a nuanced interpretation of the sculpture.

> *I have seen this sculpture and I find it awesome and inspiring. I know it has been thought to be "controversial," and I find it difficult to understand why this should be so. The sculptor, through showing Woman in the form of the Cross, is, I believe, attempting to portray women's pain, throughout history. To me it is a profound statement of faith and affirmation. She is not portraying Our Lord, per se, but rather expressing a deep feeling for the anguish and also the strength of women, and in my view, the sense that there is a female aspect of the Holy Spirit.* [14]

Laurence had already mused on the possibility of a female Christ. *The Christmas Birthday Story* tells us that Mary and Joseph did not mind at all whether their baby "turned out to be a boy or girl. Either would be fine with them." In another book, *The Fire Dwellers*, a young mother carries on a running conversation with God.

> *Listen here, God, don't talk to me like that. You have no right. You try bringing up four kids. Don't tell me you've brought up countless millions because I don't buy that. We've brought our own selves up and precious little help we've had from you. If you're there. Which probably you aren't, although I'm never convinced totally, one way or another. So next time you send somebody down here, get It born as a her with seven*

young or a him with a large family and a rotten boss, eh? Then we'll see how the inspirational bit goes.[15]

Margaret Laurence reminded me to reread her short story *The Merchant of Heaven*, when controversy was raging over the *Crucified Woman*. The story is set in a village in Ghana and tells about the efforts of a new missionary, Brother Lemon, who claimed that his business was "with the salvation of their immortal souls. That, and that alone. It's the greatest kindness I can do these people."[16] And Brother Lemon was in a hurry to get on with his mission; he wanted a thousand souls within six months. Danso, an artist who lived in the village, said, "It must be quite a procedure – to tear the soul out of a living body and throw the inconvenient flesh away like a fruit rind."[17] But Danso painted a picture for the new church.

It was a picture of the Nazarene. Danso had not portrayed any emaciated mauve-veined ever-sorrowful Jesus. This man had the body of a fisherman or a carpenter. He was well built. He had strong wrists and arms. His eyes were capable of laughter. Danso had shown Him with a group of beggars, sore-fouled, their mouths twisted in perpetual leers of pain.[18]

And he was African. The white missionary

blinked . . . sagged as though he had been struck and – yes – hurt. The old gods he could fight ... but this was a threat he had never anticipated. . . . Do many – do all of you – see Him like that? He didn't wait for an answer.[19]

Some people said, "Don't you know that Jesus was a man?" Yes, indeed Jesus was a man and he was a Jew. Artists have sometimes presented the Christ figure as African, Asian, and Native American, but more often white. Always as a man, seldom as a Jew. So finally, the question surfaces: Why not as a woman?

A crucified woman is in fact found in American literature – and she is Jewish. In Chaim Potok's novel *My Name is Asher Lev*, a young orthodox Jewish boy passionately studies art in opposition to his upbringing and his father's intentions for him. His teacher said, "I am not telling you to paint crucifixions. I am telling you that you must understand what a crucifixion is in art if you want to be a great artist."[20] Finally he painted the anguish and torment of crucifixion. There was no cross there either, but rather a venetian blind.

I drew my mother in her housecoat, with her arms extended along the horizontal of the blind, her wrists tied to it with the cords of the blind, her legs tied at the ankles to the verticle of the inner frame with another section of the cord of the blind. I arched her body and twisted her head. I drew my father standing to her right, dressed in a hat and coat and carrying an attache case. I drew myself standing to her left, dressed in paint-splattered clothes and a fisherman's cap and holding a palette and a long spearlike brush. . . . I split my mother's head into segments, some looking at me, one looking at my father, one looking upward. The torment, the tearing anguish I felt in her, I put into her mouth, into the twisting curve of her head, the arching of her slight body, the clenching of her small fists, the taut downward pointing of her thin legs. . . . For all the pain you suffered, my mama. . . . For all the anguish this picture of pain will cause you. . . . For the unspeakable mystery that brings good fathers and sons into the world and lets a mother watch them tear at each other's throats. For the Master of the Universe, whose suffering world I do not comprehend.[21]

Asher Lev's *Brooklyn Crucifixion* caused great pain to his family and synagogue. But his teacher said, "Be a great painter Asher Lev.... That will be the only justification for all the pain your art will cause." [22]

In both the written and the visual arts, an imagination is at work that connects itself with our own imagination, our fears and our hopes. Like a rainbow that appears in the sky when the rain and the sun interact together, a new reality is created – new creation and hope. Scary stuff, but without art, our lives are diminished.

Chapter Five

Woman's Body
and the Incarnation:
Mixed Messages

The Incarnation is central to Christian faith as a way of understanding and speaking about God: God as human being. The Word becoming flesh means the taking on of all humanity, all flesh, female and male. Christianity does not denigrate the body. Coming into the world as a human being is God's gift to us.

Much has been made of the importance of the empty cross for Protestant theology, because Protestants have been particularly conscious of the danger of idolatry. But the empty cross can also become an idol and can work against the meaning of the Incarnation. The empty cross in and of itself does not speak of resurrection. Protestants *interpret* the empty cross as connecting resurrection and crucifixion.

Paul says, "Yet not I live but Christ lives in me." Would not reason enable us to know that this is the witness of every Christian, that Christ lives in Paul, in us, in both female and male? Cliff Elliott of Bloor Street United pondered some of the responses made by church people to the sculpture, and he realized that the teaching of the church must in some way have

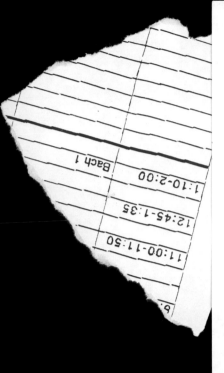

left people with limited understandings of the Incarnation.

> *When people were shocked that a* woman *was depicted as crucified and concluded that we were implying that Jesus was a woman, we realized that in our teaching of the Incarnation we had implied that to become human was to become male. This not only denied the total personality of God, with female and male characteristics; it also denied that God could be expressed in the form of a woman as well as of a man. Jesus was a man. True. But* the Christ *could have been a woman. That obvious truth some could not see. It offended others. It excited many.*

> *The shock many felt at the nakedness of the sculpture showed us that as Christians we had implied, if not actually taught, that the human body is evil. Many kept referring to "that nude statue." They saw it as a deliberate sexual titillation. They failed to see the difference between nudity, as an obsession with sex, and nakedness which is our natural state. They failed to see nakedness as a condition of vulnerability and need. They forgot Jesus' words: "I was hungry and you fed me, I was naked and you clothed me."*[23]

However, there was also evidence in some of the responses of people connecting their understanding of Incarnation with the *Crucified Woman*. Perhaps the sculpture enabled them to put their thoughts and feelings into words.

> *An important symbol for our time: the woman, the mother, the lover, pain and ecstasy at the same time. That is what the Incarnation is about, surely.*

ૠ ૠ ૠ

Says something radical, something Incarnational. Christ's suffering on the cross orients us to consider women's suffering now. Jesus Christ identified with women. Crucified Woman convicts us of our inner alienation and social alienation and yet is grand news in that God is involved in the whole of humanity.

The obvious nakedness of the woman's body in the sculpture did indeed cause consternation. The attention given to the nakedness indicates ambivalence in our culture about the female body, and for a variety of reasons. Ambivalence can be discerned in both men and women, in different ways. Some found the nakedness to be erotic and therefore in conflict with expectations about "religious" art. One person said,

Why eroticism? Eroticism is insulting, contradicts the teaching of the Church, an insulting contradiction of the Godhead. Some might be able to accept woman as crucified but not woman with such obvious sexuality.

Another person said, "The sculpture forces one to regard, not only traditional Christian imagery, but sexuality as well."

One response showed male realization of what women may have experienced throughout the ages: "For the first time I experienced what it meant to have a Christ figure that was really sexually attractive. I wanted to reach out and embrace Christ."

Another response indicated an ability to recognize and name an unexpected connection: "The tautness and intensity of anguish. Somehow the erect nipples seem to be a part of this."

Culture in general and, more specifically, the Christian faith gives women mixed messages about their bodies, and the time has come when women are refusing to accept some of these messages. Rather than face the power of women's sexuality as being equal to their own, men have traditionally tried to divide and conquer so that they had mistresses for the pleasures of the mind, prostitutes for the pleasures of the body, and wives to bear them sons. In greater numbers, women are now declining to choose between being a capricious playmate or a sexless comrade who regrets her female body as she tries to model herself on her male colleague.

It is not insignificant that it is in the ministry as a profession that sex-role stereotyping breaks down in such painful ways. A profession that has excluded women so vindictively still seems to expect women to sacrifice their sexuality by hiding their female bodies and not having babies. At the same time, many of the qualities or characteristics required of those in ministry are those of the nurturing, caring person, a role that culture has assigned to women.

While The United Church of Canada celebrated the fiftieth anniversary of the ordination of women in 1986, not a lot of attention has been paid to the fact that ordination, in 1936, was reserved for celibate women. It was not until the 1960s that married women were ordained. In the forties and fifties, they were rejected as candidates for ordination. Contrast this with school teaching, where maternity leave has been available for nearly forty years. Theologically educated women who chose to be married were described as having "chosen" not to be ordained. Social conditioning made it difficult for women to choose both marriage and ordered ministry. But the church made it impossible by refusing to ordain married women.

Ironically, the work place for male ministers is not a man's world, except when they get together as a professional group. They do most of the work of the church in the company of women, but many of the women do not feel entirely trusted. Clergymen do go to women's prayer meetings because as one of them said about a hundred years ago, "You can never tell what women might take to praying about if left alone."[24]

American theologian Dr. Edwina Hunter, in her reflective article on the *Christa*, the female crucifix sculpted by Edwina Sandys of the United States, says that the "Christ in women" is precisely what the religious establishment seeks to crucify. As an example of this, she turns to the "irregular ordination" of eleven women to the Episcopal priesthood in 1974. As male priests tried to reach a decision about the ordination of women, they said these things about the women:

> "*in a masculine role, women will become incurably frigid ... incurably promiscuous ... or destructive"* ... "*bitchy and greedy*" ... "*violent; and associated with disease*" ... "*vehicles for guilt and disillusionment*" ... "*woman nudges us into world, flesh, and even, sometimes, the territory of the devil*" ... "*prostitute*" ... "*a charming seductive exterior*"[25]

Such things have been said throughout history. Tertullian, one of the respected church fathers, said,

> *How bold these heretical women are: they have no modesty; they are bold enough to teach, to argue, to perform exorcisms, to undertake cures, and many even to baptize!*[26]

And yet theology changes over the years, sometimes presenting differently nuanced understandings, other times offering radically changed meanings. But misogyny has been pervasive in traditional theological thought. One of the most influential Protestant theologians of the twentieth century, Karl Barth, reinforces patriarchy as sanctioned by God. Barth carefully notes that the hierarchical relationship between men and women does not mean simply that woman should subordinate herself to man, but rather that both man and woman must subordinate themselves to a hierarchical order established by God, which places man under God and woman under man. For Protestants, Barth's argument, based on his interpretation of one of the Genesis accounts of creation, carries the strongest sanction: God's order. I think it is the strongest argument for patriarchy and requires the most radical rejection by theologians today.[27]

Contemporary Catholic theologian Rosemary Radford Ruether sees a non-hierarchical relationship between women and men.

> *Christ is not necessarily male, nor is the redeemed community only women, but a new humanity, female and male.... Christ, as redemptive person and Word of God, is not to be encapsulated "once-for-all" in the historical Jesus. The Christian community continues Christ's identity. As vine and branches Christic personhood continues in our sisters and brothers ... we can encounter Christ in the form of our sister.*[28]

When women and men do abandon gender prejudice and face each other, the demons of silence, contempt, jealousy, and aggressiveness come out from all around. It takes grace and a great deal of courage to anticipate the personal and public conflict that surfaces when women are valued and are no longer exploited or trivialized, or accused of stirring up trouble about something that is not important, meaning themselves! But that is the form that men's gift of love to women must take today; men must willingly live with those personal and public difficulties. And the sculpture of the *Crucified Woman* did bring out controversy. One interpretation of conflicted feelings came from a man:

> *I want to protect her – she's so vulnerable. At the same time, I'm accused and guilty, for I crucify her. I see my own cowardly violence exposed beneath all my attempts at self-deception. I long for forgiveness and peace. I wish we didn't have to go through all this controversy and conflict but I know we do.*

The women's movement has identified and openly dealt with the need for women to talk about their bodies. Rather than controlling or being controlled by them, women want to know how they work and how to care for them. Women reject, clearly and firmly, any outside control of their bodies, whether that means arbitrary sexual access or control over abortion. One response to the sculpture was

> *When I look at her body I see my own body. My own body? I've always tried to make my body fit the fantasies of others. I've wanted to be proud of my body, but really I've been ashamed of my body. Does God care about my body?*

The language of control and ownership of one's body, whether by others, the self, or by God, is not as helpful as the language of care.

Women are discovering new ways of understanding their sexuality, ways that are not derived from male understandings.

One of the consequences of this is the emergence of words and of more accurate ways of speaking while understanding that the body cannot be separated from sexual and emotional meanings. Our culture, as well as attempting to alienate women from caring for their own bodies, has expected women to care for the bodies of others – not only babies and children, but also the sick and the elderly. In determining what it needed from women, dominant culture projected some of its most problematic requirements. Women have a lot of experience in caring for the bodies of others. Even brewing the office coffee is related to bodily needs!

Some of the unsolved problems of our culture and, particularly, of our church are hidden in our language. Inclusive language is more than non-sexist. Logical, abstract language, such as that used for God by Aquinas ("Being Itself," "The First Mover," and "Pure Act"), is non-sexist but also non-relational. Language, if it is to help the mind connect with actual experience and thus enable creativity to flourish, must be our own. Finding the words to say what we mean is not only the work of toddlers and patients in a psychiatrist's office but the work of every human being. Why do we make it hard for one another? One woman wrote:

> *I keep looking at that naked body and I don't know what I should be thinking. . . . I don't know what words to use . . . tears came to my eyes. So many people in the church are upset about it. But I feel peaceful and clean, or healed, less burdened. Although I'm really quite an old woman, I feel new. I wonder if that's what people mean when they say they've been born again?*
>
> *I've never talked to anyone in the church about God, or about*

myself either, especially not about my body.

Birth control, as it developed in the sixties, offered choice concerning pregnancy to many women. But rather than welcoming the possibility of a more thoughtful caring for the reproductive systems of women, some people in our culture and in the church acted as if women could not be trusted: there might be no more babies.

Sociology teaches us how important consensual validation is in our self-understanding. Knowing our impact on others through honest dialogue enables creative change to take place. We can help each other. At Emmanuel College, many women students, and some men, came to my office, needing urgently to talk about themselves, their faith, and how to talk to others who were close to them. They wanted to know whether other people felt the same way or thought the same way. The need for validation, for talking, arose when students overheard negative comments about the sculpture.

Many women students find it difficult to believe in their own ability. Women have been seen to be well adjusted in society and well liked in the church if they adopt qualities of submissiveness, passivity, docility and dependency. Since theology is always contextual, these values are clearly established in Christian doctrine. One student at Emmanuel said of the sculpture, "Feminism gone wild! Women trying to be men." But any change causes the whole system to move. One woman said,

> *When I was looking at the sculpture, I met another woman there, and we started talking about it. I didn't know what to think, but she really liked it. I learned a lot from her. Most of all I decided if she can talk like that, I can too.*

The female body has been assumed to be "less" than the male body. Freud contributed the notion of "penis envy" to our conceptual vocabulary. This means that little girls see the male penis as something their own bodies lack. There certainly is something that women are missing – economic, political, and social power! It is the power that women envy, not the penis, although they do seem to go together. Rather than experiencing the female body as deficient, many women feel that the reproductive system is an addition to the female body. How to care for the reproductive system is still problematic. Anatomy both is and is not destiny. The female body is more than a reproductive system, but there is a reproductive system that requires care and decisions; it may cause sadness or it may bring joy. Women give their bodies when they give birth, when they choose to become pregnant.

Some women choose not to become pregnant. Others may choose abortion rather than the continuance of an unwanted pregnancy. The concept of abortion, meaning as it does, "induced miscarriage," is one that we could live without. Medical intervention can take place when the menstrual period is delayed, whether by fertilization of the ovum or by another cause. Women should not have to wait until they know that they are pregnant before taking action to induce their period. Drugs are available for female athletes, whose performance would be limited by the retention of menstrual fluids in the body. The comfort of any woman is important. Thorough medical research should take place on the widespread use of the drug that is used in "morning after pills." If a woman does not want to be pregnant, she should be able to ensure that she is not and not have to wait for weeks until the termination of the pregnancy becomes more physically difficult, expensive, emotionally distressing, and morally uncertain.

Many women are delighted when they are no longer pregnant, but some women have feelings that are often labelled as "guilt." In the maternity ward, after a healthy and much-wanted baby is born, many women experience a mild form of post-partum depression due to hormonal change. The feeling subsides quickly and women are emotionally supported during that time. Post-partum depression has the same characteristics as the so-called "guilt" of the woman who has had an abortion. No one can distinguish between mild depression and guilt. Why has the notion of guilt been evoked? Words are powerful, and some words can oppress.

The part of the creation story that has come to be known as the Fall has been used to put women in double jeopardy. First of all there is an implicit notion of gravity: that the body fell faster and farther than the mind. We have long been bombarded by the notion that woman is body and man is mind. It is interesting to imagine Christian theology without a doctrine of the Fall. The word "fall" is not in the biblical text. Is it a curse to acquire knowledge, develop a sense of freedom and responsibility, and to long for relationship? Something was lost and something was gained. Most of all, perhaps the story has to do with broken relationships.

Original Sin, a doctrine that interprets sin as more than conscious choice, is a helpful way of expressing the distorted dimension of the world into which all of us are born. But women have been accused of introducing sin into the world. There is too much negative attention to the female body in the notion of the Fall. If pain in childbirth is the organizing principle, then all female mammals must have "fallen" as well.

The idea that woman is body and man is mind appears every now and then in both religion and culture. Women's bodies have to bear too much responsibility. Women are conditioned to believe that human love is dependent on a "perfect" female body. The notion that a woman's value is based exclusively on her body creates feelings of alienation and exploitation within her.

All of us come to God in our bodies; God came to us in a body. Our hope is in the resurrection of the body. If we are to receive these gifts, we may have to pay attention to the body in ways that are neither exploitative nor manipulative. Outside of family life, we are nearly always stingy with our bodies. Touch is one of the forms that the healing ministry requires. "I was touched by that," we sometimes say. Jesus asked, "Who touched me?" Jesus was forever reaching out and touching someone. People were reaching out to touch him. Touch, the laying on of hands, can be loving and healing, or it can be hating and hurting. Touch is powerful.

The closest body relationship that is possible is in the experience of pregnancy, childbirth, and lactation. It is not always wonderful, but it is close. All of us are born into the world having literally lived inside another person. The one in whom we live and move and have our being is a way of speaking about God as womb, as pregnant woman, as dwelling place, as mother.

Naming God as Mother is not as common as naming God as Father. We do both today. The Bible uses both metaphors, but the church has spoken of God as Father rather relentlessly and exclusively. In Isaiah, we can read that God goes into labour.

Now I will cry out like a woman in travail, I will gasp and pant (42:14).

Shall I bring to the birth and not cause to bring forth? says

*the Lord; shall I, who cause to bring forth, shut the womb?
(66:9).*

Isaiah also sees God as a remembering, loving, and comforting Mother.

*Can a woman forget her sucking child that she should have
no compassion on the son of her womb? Even these may
forget, yet I will not forget you (49:15).*

*As one whom his mother comforts, so will I comfort you
(66:13).*

In the New Testament, there is an image of Jesus as a hen gathering her chicks under her wing (Matthew 23:37), and there is a parable of God as a woman searching for her lost coin (Luke 15: 8-9). Female images of God do not seem to be as familiar as male images.

The sculpture asks us to ask the question: Why do we have so much language about God as Father? Father is a wonderful image for God, but why has it become so literal? The fact is that the metaphor of God as Father has become empty and hurtful to many women and men. Through the repeated use of God the Father, in our minds God becomes male and therefore male becomes God, and so on. The Bible also uses the metaphor of God as Mother and God as Lover. We can hardly do better than that! God as Mother, Father, Lover, knowing us, loving us, understanding us, and accepting us, knowing what we need before we ask and numbering the very hairs of our heads, like a mother who strokes her baby's head, like lovers who run their fingers through each other's hair.

The image of God as Pregnant Woman or as Mother

reminds us that the body of a woman can feed another human being. The mother literally feeds the hungry one. Lactation combines the power and ability to do something about hunger with a willingness and desire to be for the other, to be good for the other. The mother gives milk to the infant, and by its very existence, the infant has brought milk to the breast.

In God's economy there is milk for every infant. The bliss of a land flowing with milk and honey could be what it means to be born into the world. God came into the world the same as every human being, hungry, looking for the mother's breast. The figure of the sculpture has small, but swollen, breasts. One person said, "The large smooth nipples are hard not to notice."

Without denying the value and joy of being a mother, the women's movement has also helped our culture to begin to understand that responsibility for the care of children and others need not be the exclusive domain of women. Human development includes the proper care and growth of all people, and all people can share in the responsibility.

It is interesting to note the different connotations associated with the words "mothering" and "fathering." Biologically, only women are mothers. But the creative acts of caring for another can be carried out by fathers, mothers, friends, and lovers. All of these are images for God. And God is also Infant.

God came into the world as an infant – born to the very self-confident young woman who sang Hannah's song. Hannah was too old to have a baby. Was Mary too young? We've called their song the Magnificat and distorted its meaning. "My soul magnifies God" – magnifies – makes bigger.

Certainly her body magnified God as it became bigger with new life. Mary, a young Jewish peasant woman, says that God has brought down rulers from their thrones but has lifted up the humble. "God has filled the hungry with good things, but has sent the rich away empty." "All generations will call me blessed" has been embalmed in a hermeneutic of humility and virginity. She sounds neither humble nor virginal! She is concerned, however, with the hungry being filled and so should we all.

Most of us realize that it is children who are the major victims of hunger and poverty. When people are hungry they must be fed, but thoughtful social assistance reviewers recommend the kind of help that enables people to make the transition from dependency to autonomy and from exclusion on the margins of society to integration within the mainstream of community life. Pastoral care and social action are not separate dimensions of Christ's ministry. Changing the structures that cause poverty, hunger, and marginalization is the first step in caring for women and children who are so overly represented in the lowest income categories.

A biblical image for God that is rarely discussed is as Midwife. Psalm 22: 9-10 says, "Yet you are the one who took me from the womb. You kept me safe upon my mother's breasts. I was cast upon you from the womb" (see also Ps. 71:6). A young Sandanista woman, Dora Maria Tellez, who worked underground for the overthrow of Nicaragua's dictator in 1979, had been a medical student. In a book by Margaret Randall, *Sandino's Daughters*, Dora tells about the first time that she assisted in the birth of a baby, as a story of cooperation with nature in bringing a new person into the world. She knows that what she is doing is important work. "It's time for me to muster my courage," she says. As the woman moans and pushes, the baby's head appears. "I'm this baby's first contact with the world of people. . . . I've done it. I've gotten the baby completely out." Her hands tremble and she feels tired, but she thinks of the world into which this baby boy has been born.

Poverty, if not outright misery, probably awaits him. In fact, he has already begun to live it. Will his body survive? And what about his hopes? Have I completed my mission by aiding his birth? I must say no. Our work will be done when we can give these young ones a new world, a different world. I must be committed to the birth of that new world, which like every birth will be painful and at the same time joyous.[29]

Women's bodies break open in childbirth. Amidst waters breaking, blood flowing, muscles contracting, pushing and moaning, new life is given: birth is a gift.

My body given for you.
My blood shed for you.

Every person born into the world has known the hospitality of a woman's body.

Chapter Six

Suffering:
Pastoral Care and
Social Action

One Emmanuel student said of the *Crucified Woman*, "She offers no word of forgiveness, no hope of reconciliation. There is no prophetic love in what she says to me, no words of gospel."

Another student replied:

No words of gospel? I long to share the word of the gospel that she has for me. When Jesus went to his death, even death on a cross, he hallowed the deaths of all victims of violence. When the Logos became flesh, God became Victim – just another victim of our innate and mysteriously demonic need to dominate and destroy. We became the Victimizer. Jesus' death is a judgment on all violence, a judgement on the creatures who put to death the One who had been with God and indeed was God from the beginning.

The Crucified Woman *does three things for me. Her form, the cruciform, haunts me as I see the image of Jesus, naked and tortured, and the image of the woman, naked and tortured, tumble over each other. She points me to Jesus, the Crucified One, the Lamb who was slain and now lives and reigns with God forever. But at the same time, she points me to all victims of violence who share in Jesus' communion of blood shed for our sins. She also of necessity points me to me. It is only the image and the heinous reality of the violent death of Jesus that has given me the tools I need to deal with the heinous reality of violence in my own life.*

Who gave my father permission to beat his own daughter – flesh of his flesh? Who gave my grandfather permission to think he could molest and tyrannize his tiny, defenceless granddaughter? And who gave permission to the stranger to think he could rape and leave me as if nothing had happened and a horrific event had not taken place? I did not – but they got it from some place – from the demonic spirit and will to dominate that contaminates and damns us all. How I have longed for the comfort that my experience was isolated, even pardonable, on the basis of insanity. It was not and is not. Their insanity was their normalcy.

It is only twelve years of intense fellowship with the Crucified Jesus that has set me on the road to healing. And only as I deal with the reality of being victim do I have the courage – even the drivenness – to reach out to other victims and to seek with them their healing.

It is the spirit of Jesus the Crucified who gives me the grace not to become victim turned victimizer and to break the cycle of violence. You see, I can identify with Jesus as Victim, and Jesus as Victim can and has identified with me. I have been touched and healed by bloodied and broken hands.

My own journey to resurrection and wholeness began at the initiative of the abused, beaten, tortured, violated Christ. "Behold, He is coming with the clouds and every eye shall see Him, every one who pierced Him," and all those who have been pierced like him shall be with him.

The saddest thing for me about the Crucified Woman is that perhaps you have to be a woman to see Christ Jesus imaged in her, our sister. . . . I bless the artist in the name of Jesus of Nazareth.

The suffering of women through sexual violence is a form of suffering that has only recently come out into the open. Women suffer in many ways, but the fact that they suffer because of physical, sexual, psychological, and economic abuse can no longer be set aside, or even more blasphemously, be seen as God's will, a notion that has been too frequently invoked as an explanation for all suffering. That kind of thinking makes God a sadist. God is on the side of the victim; the God that is revealed in Jesus Christ is a God that suffers, not a God that causes suffering.

Dorothee Soelle, in her book *Suffering*, tells the story of a woman who lives in a Catholic village in Austria. The woman stays on and on in a marriage, although the relationship with her husband is intolerable. He beats her physically, tortures her mentally, humiliates her, scorns her, and maligns her before friends and family. She endures this hell, but as she walks beside the river, she wishes she were lying in it. She wonders about suicide, but she can not do that because of her children. She can not consider divorce. Her neighbours are outraged by the way her husband treats her, but everyone in the village, including the woman herself, is caught in some notion of the omnipotence of God, a notion that everything that happens is God's will, a pietistic fatalism that leads to a numbing acceptance of needless suffering.

Fortunately, talking about God in terms of power is becoming rarer. Douglas Hall, in his book *God and Human Suffering*, speaks of

> *situations where power is of no avail.* They are most of the situations in which as human beings we find ourselves! *May we not also dare to say that, from the standpoint of a faith tradition which posits love, not power, as God's primary perfection, they are most of the situations in which God finds God's Self too?*[30]

It is important for us to distinguish as clearly as we can between needless suffering, which can be prevented, and the kind of suffering that is part of what it means to be human. Physical suffering, pain, injury, and deterioration is a condition of creatureliness shared with all other animals that have a central nervous system. The suffering that women experience as victims of sexual violence is needless suffering.

So much has been written by theologians and creative writers about suffering. Theology has changed recently in its under-standing of God as a God who suffers. Patripassionism (the belief that God suffers) was originally a heresy. But now theologians write about God suffering with us. One dark rainy night, a car with faulty windshield wipers skidded on an icy patch of road without guard rails and slipped into the river. The young man driving the car died. His father, the Reverend William Sloane Coffin, speaking of his own grief in a sermon at Riverside Church in New York City, said, "When the icy waters covered the car that night, God's heart was the first of all our hearts to break."

And there is the suffering of poverty and starvation. Once again we see the bodies of emaciated and dying children in Ethiopia. Some people ask, "Why does God let this happen?" God might well be asking, "Why do *you* let this happen?" Surely we deny God's hope for us in our unwillingness to actually care for God's created world, including each other. I find it quite possible to connect our exploitation and abuse of the environment with our exploitation and abuse of women. Somewhere in the development of Christian thought, the insistence that God is a God of history, not a God of nature, led us to "conquer and subdue" the earth, rather than care for it. And we have connected women with nature. Women have been treated like the environment, possessed, exploited, and subordinated.

Our health care system understands that preventative health care *is* health care. In the church, we have polarized social action and pastoral care, rather than understanding social action as preventative pastoral care. Social action has been thought of as public whereas pastoral care has been thought of as private. This distinction has not been helpful for women, since sexual behaviours have been considered private matters and abused women seen as private patients. Social action to prevent sexual violence against women and children is *caring* for women. We should not separate pastoral care and social action. The particular suffering of women through sexual violence shows clearly that pastoral care and social action are not separate ways of carrying out Christ's ministry; both are healing ministries.

A violent assault made headlines around the world on December 6, 1989, when fourteen young women, engineering students, were shot to death at Ecole Polytechnique in Montreal. The killer, who also killed himself, blamed feminists for the misfortunes of his life. Newscasters said he was psychotic, and no doubt he was, but in directing his hate and violence against women, he simply escalated and drew media attention to what is an everyday occurrence.

A newspaper article entitled "Killings of Women are 'routine,'"[31] points out that in one summer month, eleven Montreal women and six of their children were killed by their husbands or sexual partners. Canadian Centre for Justice statistics show that almost half of all murders are the result of domestic violence. And that does not include the violence, including murders, that occurs outside of live-in relationships.

Some people described the Montreal massacre as an isolated incident, the act of a madman. However, Ursula Franklin, Professor Emeritus of the Faculty of Applied Science and Engineering in the University of Toronto, addressed that understanding in a speech. She said,

> Yes . . . but it is not unrelated to what is going on around us. That people get mad may happen in any society, any place, every place. But how people get mad, how that escalation from prejudice to hate to violence occurs, what and who is hated, how it is expressed, is not unrelated to the world around us.

> When a madman uses easily available weapons and easily available prejudices, it is not totally his problem that will go away when he goes away. At another time it could have been Jews who were lined up, it could have been black people, but in Montreal they were women, and they were women in an engineering faculty. Killed by somebody who wanted to be an engineer.[32]

Memorial services were held all across Canada. In Toronto, the *Crucified Woman* was the place in the hearts and minds of women to gather and meet together in that strange mixture of grief, anger, sorrow, rage, and mourning. About 500 people gathered, some to pray, many to weep. Several people brought flowers. Red roses and red carnations were placed at the base of the sculpture. The vigil, held at noon on the day after the massacre, was covered by all major television networks, radio stations, and newspapers. One journalist described the location as "around an unbearably poignant sculpture of a naked crucified woman."[33]

Dr. Eva Kushner, president of Victoria University, spoke in French, extending sympathy to the parents, husbands, friends, and colleagues of the dead women.

Dr. Nancy Jackman, feminist activist and one of the organizers of the vigil, passed a crystal chalice of red wine and said,

> *We begin to understand why women are murdered. It's because we create life. It's because we have the blood of life in our bodies that our blood is wasted in murder. Let us pledge today, in the pre-patriarchal women's ritual of communion, that the blood of the women of Montreal will not be wasted. Let us take this communion, representing their blood, mixing their blood with ours, sisters to sisters. Let it strengthen us in our fight against hatred, against violence, and against the murder of women.*

Men were welcomed as they joined the women there, singing feminist songs. Columnist Michele Landsberg wrote of "generous adult intelligent men who utterly reject violence, who are revolted by macho sexism in jokes or entertainment, who believe passionately in human equality." She said,

We must all stand together, like the Danes putting on yellow armbands in defiance of Hitler's round-up of the Jews, and say "we are all feminists: we stand for an end to woman-hating violence in words, in pictures, in deeds."[34]

It was a bitterly cold winter day. In winter the sculpture is starkly visible, no longer surrounded by the soft green leaves of the birches in spring, nor the deep golden leaves of autumn. The feeling of being abandoned and vulnerable was shared and talked about and yet all were standing together, committed to the end of the needless suffering of women. The sense of community was strong.

Other services have been held at the place where the sculpture now stands on the Emmanuel College grounds. On Easter Morning 1989, ten years after the *Crucified Woman* came to Bloor Street Church, an early service was arranged by Bloor Street people. Early on that first day of the week, while it was yet dark, we trudged to the garden, still needing boots in the chilly dampness of April. The service was short. A litany gave participants an opportunity to name women whose lives should be particularly remembered that day. Many spoke of mothers and grandmothers, remembering with gratitude a past that strengthened them. But Helga Kutz Harder thought of her broken history and the loss of her own future. She spoke of her daughter Naomi, who had been killed by a gun held by her former boyfriend José, a Salvadoran refugee. He shot himself after he shot her. Naomi was a twenty-one-year-old university student, home for Christmas holidays.

Commitment to social justice had led Naomi to live and work in Zaire and Nicaragua. Respect for her mother's work with refugees led Naomi to volunteer to work with refugees in Toronto. In that context she met José and worked with him on Tools for Peace. A relationship of love had grown between them, but the time had come for Naomi to tell José that the relationship was over.

Many people were anxious to explain and understand why José could not cope with life and love in his new country, but Helga felt that no one had named the evil. Naomi died because she was a woman. As Helga looked at the *Crucified Woman*, she saw a young woman's body broken and blood shed. When Helga takes communion with the whole company of heaven, one of that company is a young fair-haired woman who died for what she believed in: social justice, honesty, and love.

The sculpture seemed to be Lent itself, for it gathered up all of the suffering, all of the pain in our lives. We brought our sorrow and our anger and our bewilderment, and we received hope. An ancient prayer says, "Suffering of Christ, strengthen me." How does that happen? Some suffering does strengthen us in that it makes us more mature and compassionate. Some people say that we learn from suffering, but other forms of suffering simply dehumanize and limit us in every way. But the suffering of Christ does indeed strengthen us in enabling us to work to prevent the suffering of others. Apathy is the inability to care about suffering.

The face of the sculpture is devoid of discernible personality: it is a face of generalized sorrow. Many people have noted the connection between the youthful quality of female beauty in the torso and the depersonalized sorrowing face. Cross-hatched grooves, which in some places emphasize contours in the body, may be reminders of the scourging of Jesus. To suggest that Jesus suffered more than others is macabre.[35] The meaning of Jesus' suffering and death is understood when the church confesses Jesus as Christ and in so doing realizes that Christ continues to suffer before our eyes.

The connection between the sorrow and pain in the face and the cultural idea of female beauty in the body is profoundly significant. Women in our culture suffer *because* of their bodies. Caring about this can become action when we confess our personal and communal responsibility for violence against women, the sin of complicity in structures and attitudes that cause needless suffering. Pastoral care takes the form of social action. We need all the intelligence, all the passion, and all the discernment we can muster to dismantle the expectations, attitudes, and structures in our society that cause needless suffering.

When we remember the suffering of Jesus Christ but stare blindly as Christ continues to suffer, we have an empty faith. The Christian faith is always political, and political structures are forever being used to confound God's gracious gift of hope. In the sixteenth century, Thomas Muntzer, the man who led the peasants' revolt in Luther's time, said "No man can tell you anything about God as long as he rules over you."

Through the sculpture, people heard God calling them to confess their oppressive power over the lives of women, to confess their complicity in the growth of the pornography in our society and in the structures of economic hardship that women endure. God does not tolerate social suffering that can be prevented. The God who is revealed to us in Jesus Christ is a God who suffers, who becomes powerless so that we may act with courage and compassion to stop the needless suffering of women.

Confession and commitment to change were expressed by both women and men.

God must be glad to have this beautiful, moving sculpture

near the cross. It helps us to remember that Jesus struggled for woman's dignity.

ﮩ ﮩ ﮩ

I felt the Crucified Woman *was magnificent – real – alive – truly woman – human – God. I saw the picture before coming and thought I would know what to expect – but I met the truly unexpected. At the same instant she called me to prayer, song, pain, weeping.*

ﮩ ﮩ ﮩ

I see it as a symbol of human suffering, which through Christ's suffering is redeemed. The crucifixion is sometimes a portrayal of an historical event and sometimes every Christian's willingness to "go to the death," "give all," "die with Christ," as a follower of Christ. I am willing to suffer as Christ suffered but no crucifixion image had me in it before.

ﮩ ﮩ ﮩ

Beautiful, powerful, a challenge to take up the cross and not be a passive bystander.

A battered wife told her social worker that when she saw the *Crucified Woman* she was able to relate to Christ for the first time. In both liturgy and Bible study, we must remember that violated women are in our midst. When women participate in biblical interpretation, we can all hear the story differently.

Imagine yourself a battered woman and listen to Psalm 55 (NIV):

My heart is in anguish within me;
the terrors of death assail me.

Fear and trembling have beset me;
horror has overwhelmed me. . . .

If an enemy were insulting me,
I could endure it;
if a foe were raising himself against me,
I could hide from him.
But it is you, a man like myself,
my companion, my close friend,
with whom I once enjoyed sweet fellowship
as we walked with the throng at the house of God. . . .

My companion attacks his friends;
he violates his covenant.
His speech is smooth as butter,
yet war is in his heart;
his words are more soothing than oil,
yet they are drawn swords. . . .

Some of the needless suffering that women endure, whether it is physical, psychological, or economic, is directly related to misogyny within the Christian church. Christian patriarchy informed the social order throughout the Christendom era. Religious tradition to a great extent justifies the psychological, economic, and physical abuse that is still the experience of many women. Augustine, whose admiration for his mother Monica is well documented, approved of her submissiveness and noted that she had escaped being beaten by her husband, whereas more assertive women had reaped a reward of curses and blows.[36] Many men interpret women's lives in exactly the same way today.

Women's suffering, women's tears. In *The Memoirs of a Survivor*, Doris Lessing wrote:

She was weeping as a woman weeps, which is to say as if the earth were bleeding. . . .

. . . it is not the pain in a woman's crying that is the point; no, it is finality of the acceptance of a wrong. So it was, is now, and must ever be, say those closed oozing eyes, the rocking body, the grief. Grief − yes, an act of mourning; that's it. [37]

Around the world, we are all one body. When some of us suffer, we all suffer. Over 100 written responses to the *Crucified Woman* were received at Bloor Street United Church, and most of them had to do with suffering. One woman wrote:

I am a Christian feminist and have experienced a lot of pain in feeling alienated and not recognized by the church. I am referring here to the use of sexist language, imagery, models of ministry, and patriarchal theology. I long for the time when my sisters and I will feel support and respect from the church. Having that beautiful sculpture − the Crucified Woman − *in front of the church on Good Friday and publicly giving support to battered women spoke to me more than you would realize. It is profoundly moving to see a female symbol as a crucifix. Women throughout the centuries have given of themselves as their way of caring − and all too often unrewarded and at great cost to all. It was very healing for me to have you recognize the pain of women.*

Another man said,

I've been listening to the way women talk about the sculpture. I didn't know women talked that way. I've never done anything terrible to women and I've never really understood what problems middle-class women thought they had. I've always liked women and tried to be courteous, but I realize now that I don't really know women. I don't know how they feel, what they talk about to each other. I've always thought women were more religious than men. I didn't ever know that they thought some of the things they're saying.

Others wrote:

I can't tell you how important this image of the Crucified Woman *is to me. I am shaken, scalded, trembling. . . . Why does it mean so much to me? Is it because I am a woman and the Church has never noticed my particular pain?*

❧ ❧ ❧

I had the opportunity to experience a visual sense of my pain. . . . while I looked at the sculpture full force, I had a great sense of pain that I had to bear because my body is female, and of the oppression I experience simply because my body is like that of the sculpture. The face was so similar to that of a battered woman that I had counselled years ago that I was startled. . . . I have a sense of your caring for me and other women, even though you do not know me.

Alice Walker's novel *The Color Purple* tells us through letters to God the story of a young black woman, a woman deceived, betrayed, abused, and whose search for God leads her to tell the truth about her life. The truth is scalding, heartbreaking, never sentimental, but resplendent with good humour and gratitude. As a teenager Celie was raped continuously by the man she thought was her father. Much later, as an adult woman, and aware at last of her own sexual feelings through her relationship with another woman, Celie listens as Shug tells her that God loves those feelings and that people who know how much God loves what God has made are able to enjoy their own sexual feelings. God is on the side of joy. In her conversation about God, Shug echoes a biblical notion that God is more generous and loving than human beings are. Why wouldn't God expect us to like what God has given us? We do not give a stone when children ask for bread. Since we give good gifts to our children, we can expect even more understanding and generosity from God (Matt. 7:11).

As Celie and Shug talk, Celie tries to accept a new understanding of God, but she knows that she has to get away from earlier understandings. Celie's first experiences of sexual behaviour had been bad news and her first image of God had been bad news. As she came to realize that loving, sexual feelings were bearers of grace and joy in her life, and were in fact blessed by God, her image of God also changed. Images of God as lover are powerful and precarious. [38]

Sexual longing and sexual intimacy are among the most important connections between human beings. But they are also areas where much can go wrong. Part of what has gone wrong for women is that male fantasies are taken as the norm. Male fantasies and fears make great literature – Othello and Hamlet, for instance – but not great lives.

There are theological questions that should be raised about marriage and about the marriage service. People want to be married. They want everyone to know about their love and their intention to take care of that love. The two people who are making the marriage promises are equally mature, responsible, and independent, and at the same time amateurs who need the support of the Christian community. The marriage service should begin with that understanding and not contradict it. The church has a great deal of responsibility for what people think about marriage. Some of the biblical imagery about marriage infantilizes women. The church as the bride of Christ perpetuates the absence of mutuality: Christ as bridegroom, always faithful, always forgiving. It is a set-up. Marriage in biblical times was an institution wherein the woman (or women) was (or were) counted among men's possessions. It is not helpful for us at this time to accept such assumptions implicitly or explicitly.

Popular theology is found in the hymns we sing. For example:

The church's one foundation
is Jesus Christ her Lord . . .

From heaven he came and sought her
to be his holy bride
With his own blood he bought her,
and for her life he died.

The absence of mutuality in marriage and the notion of bride as possession are unhelpful understandings of marriage. The church has perpetuated sexist traditions in the marriage service itself, notably in treating the bride and groom differently.

Often the bride is still "given" in marriage from one man (her father) to another (the bridegroom).

Brides often carry on this tradition, ignoring its historical roots, as a way of "honouring" their fathers. They think their fathers expect this. If their consciousness is raised at a later date, they will realize how much they have dishonoured themselves, their mothers, and their husbands. The father of the bride also may regret his role in an empty ritual. New rituals that recognize mutuality, humility, compassion, and support are needed both for the couple and for their families and friends.

In April 1979, while the *Crucified Woman* was there, my daughter Catherine was married in Bloor Street United Church. Like many other mothers of the bride, I was tired from wedding preparations, but I was also enlivened by the love and joy all around me. Controversy about the sculpture had begun to subside, but I was tired from all of that too, as well as strengthened and deeply moved by how much the sculpture meant to people. Loneliness washed softly over me as I remembered my own April wedding twenty-five years earlier. Catherine's father had died when she was two. Catherine and Paul walked down the aisle together, turned to face a congregation of supportive and loving friends and family, and made promises to love and to be faithful to each other. Afterwards someone said to me, "You know, I had wondered who would give Catherine away. But I liked it this way. The bride doesn't have to be given away by anyone, does she?" And I answered, "No, she doesn't."

Every now and then in social and political structures, in relationships with those with whom I live, love, and work, and in myself, I glimpse a new creation. I believe that she will be blessed who believes there shall be a performance of those things that were told her from God; that the proud in the imagination of their hearts will be scattered, the mighty will be put down from their seats, the hungry will be filled with good things, and all generations will call woman *blessed*.

For reflection, conversation, or discussion

Chapter One

Celebration and Controversy: In the Church

1. For many people the sculpture has caused controversy, confusion, change, and also growth in the faith. Can you remember times in your life when crisis and controversy led to growth in your faith?

2. What does it mean to you that a congregation is experienced in relating the arts to education and worship? How do you connect such an interest to the church's mission? How might your church go about encouraging commitment to the arts?

3. Discussion took place in the congregation before the decision was made to place the sculpture in the chancel. What points of view and concerns might have been put forth?

4. What does "patriarchal theology" mean? Talk about its characteristics. How have women been silenced by such theology? How have you been silenced? How have men benefited from such theology? How would men benefit by inclusive theology?

5. Think of a time when you have felt mute or paralysed. What could have helped you to act or speak? Where do you need a voice or movement now? Can you ask for what you need?

Chapter Two

Celebration and Controversy: In the University

1. Look at the words of the hymn "Re-membering," written by Sylvia Dunstan. Sing or read the words aloud. What is there about the hymn that makes it traditional? What is there about it that makes it inclusive?

2. How would a "resurrection of female worth" look and feel in your life? As a woman? As a man?

3. In what way is the preparation and serving of food an ambiguous symbol for women? Do you experience that sense of ambiguity? Share some of your stories about the preparation of food (both men and women). Have you felt exploitation, ingratitude, joy, celebration, achievement, cooperation? What other feelings? Read Luke 10:38-42. The story of Mary and Martha has been interpreted in many ways. There is evidence that this is a post-resurrection

story that has been put into the life of Jesus by the editors. Martha may have been deacon in the new church and engaged in the serving of a Eucharistic meal. How does that change your understanding of this passage?

4. At the inter-faith conference, women talked to each other about the things "they like to tell each other if left on their own." If you have seen the film *The Company of Strangers*, you have seen women talking to each other honestly and openly about themselves. In what way is such conversation "religious"?

5. If you had been a member of the Senate of Victoria University, how would you respond to the report of the Senate Art Committee?

6. Look at the questions that the students in the aesthetics class were given. Which responses are the most interesting to you? How do you respond to the questions: Is it art? Is it religious?

7. Can you think of resurrection in your own life as you live it? Are new understanding, new perception, new relationships ways of discerning resurrection in your life? Can you share stories of resurrection in your life?

Chapter Three

Artistic and Theological Differences: A Transforming Story

1. What are your earliest memories of the ways crucifixion is

portrayed? Did your understanding of it change? Can you talk about your memories and views of crucifixion? How are you affected by the differences between traditional portrayals and the *Crucified Woman*?

2. Do you see yourself or someone you know in the *Crucified Woman*? How? Meditate on the feelings you have. Perhaps you would write a poem, a prayer, or draw a picture to express your feelings. Talk about some of the feelings and insights you have about the ways the sculpture can connect women's lives with the Christian story.

3. Read the comments. Which ones speak directly to you? What would you have said?

4. Read I Peter 2:24. How have you found healing "by his wounds"? What scars do you bear that tell a resurrection story?

5. What experiences do you have of women's theology?

6. How does reading this chapter affect your understanding of crucifixion, suffering, resurrection, Protestantism, or our Jewish roots?

7. Use art materials, body sculpture, or words to portray the wounded or suffering person in your own life story.

    Share what you wish about your portrayal, and reflect on your own insights and on the response of others. How was this process a way of doing theology?

Chapter Four

Protestantism and Art: A Conflicted Relationship

1. What do you think of the assertion that art is a prophetic reflection and, as such, an agent that compels creative change? Can you think of experiences where art brought about creative change?

2. Art and beauty have traditionally been connected. Does art have to be beautiful? How has the meaning of beautiful become established and changed in your understanding?

3. Different kinds of "sacrifice" are seen in the story *Babette's Feast*. When does sacrifice seem to be for the sake of goodness? How has self-sacrifice led to diminished lives for women? What stories from your own life or the lives of others deal with choices to give up something? What conditions create a "free" choice? What are the hazards for women in making choices?

4. "Artistic ways of knowing are not literal." Which biblical expressions or images that are not literal come to your mind?

5. Have you seen artistic expressions of Christ as African, Asian, or Native American? Do you have a memory of the first time you saw such an image? Do such experiences help in the universalizing of the gospel?

6. Change sometimes causes pain and pain sometimes causes change. Can you remember times of emotional, social, or

spiritual change in your life? Were there struggles or controversy associated with this change?

Chapter Five

Woman's Body and the Incarnation: Mixed Messages

1. Who is Jesus for you today? Do you respond more to images like brother or friend or to Lord and Saviour? Do you know Jesus as healer? As servant? As liberator? Could Jesus be your sister? Your lover?

2. In her book, *Sexism and God Talk*, theologian Rosemary Radford Ruether says, "Christ is not necessarily male, nor is the redeemed community only women, but a new humanity, female and male. . . . Christ, as redemptive person and Word of God, is not to be encapsulated "once-for-all" in the historical Jesus. The Christian community continues Christ's identity. As vine and branches Christic personhood continues in our sisters and brothers. . . . we can encounter *Christ in the form of our sister*." Talk about what this kind of "Christology" means for you.

3. Some people found the nakedness of the sculpture to be erotic. Have you had experiences where people thought that the erotic and the religious must be separated?

4. Are there parts of your body that you are ashamed of? What other feelings besides shame, embarrassment, betrayal, and humour seem to be present? What early memories do you have of needing to hide parts of your body?

5. Do you know stories of your own birth? Have your parents talked to you about your birth? If you have been pregnant, can you tell stories of your pregnancy and childbirth as theology?

Chapter Six

Suffering: Pastoral Care and Social Action

1. What words of gospel - good news - do you hear from the *Crucified Woman*?

2. Read Luke 10:29-37. Re-read it changing the victim to a woman - perhaps a waitress coming home late at night, who is sexually assaulted near her home. Who is the priest? Who is the Levite? Who is the Samaritan?

3. It is not easy to know how to respond to sexual violence. Talk about how a community of faith could work to bring justice and healing to victims and to the larger society. How can a congregation respond individually and collectively to victims, families, and victimizers?

4. Read Psalm 55 and respond to it out of your own experience. Imagine yourself a battered woman and respond. Write a psalm or prayer of your own.

5. Read Genesis 2:22-24. What happens when bone and flesh are battered or killed? What does this passage mean to you?

6. Read Ephesians 5:22-24. This is part of a household code

which prescribes behaviour in a clearly patriarchal order in which the wife is subordinate. If this is seen in the context of Christian love (Mark 12:31), does the meaning change for you?

7. Read Mark 2:23-28. How does recalling Jesus and the Sabbath help us to view marriage? In the past, the church has tacitly supported wife abuse by its insistence that marriages must be maintained at all costs. Talk about how the church as God's people can find new life and resurrection in this situation.

8. If you have been married, what do you remember about the marriage service? What would you like to have been different? Are there other things about your wedding that seemed "not you"? What did you need at this time that you did not have?

Notes

1. Clifford Elliott, "Crucified Woman," *Exchange* (The United Church of Canada, Winter 1982): 20.

2. Dorothee Soelle, *Suffering* (Philadelphia: Fortress Press, 1975), 85.

3. Paul Tillich, "Existentialist Aspects of Modern Art" in *Christianity and the Existentialists*, ed. Carl Michalson (New York: Charles Scribner's Sons, 1956), 138.

4. Film: *Camille Claudel*, dir. Bruno Nuytten, France, 1989.

5. The story can be found in Isak Dinesen, *Anecdotes of Destiny* (New York: Random House, 1958). The film *Babette's Feast*, dir. Gabriel Axel, Denmark, 1987, is available in video.

6. *Anecdotes of Destiny*, 37.

7. Ibid., 50-51.

8. Ibid., 68.

9. *Luther's Works*: Weimar edition, 16, 437

10. Quoted by Bobbie Crawford, "A Female Crucifix," in *Daughters of Sarah*, Vol. 14, No. 6 (November/December 1988, Chicago): 26.

11. Ibid., 27.

12. Quoted by Michael J. Farrell, "Christa," in *National Catholic Reporter*, (April 5, 1985): 12.

13. Carter Heyward, *Touching our Strength* (San Francisco: Harper Collins Publishers, 1989), 117.

14. Margaret Laurence, personal letter to author.

15. Margaret Laurence, *The Fire Dwellers* (Toronto: McClelland & Stewart, 1973), 168.

16. Margaret Laurence, "The Merchant of Heaven," in *The Tomorrow Tamer* (Toronto: McClelland & Stewart, 1970), 58.

17. Ibid., 74.

18. Ibid., 75-76.

19. Ibid., 76.

20. Chaim Potok, *My Name is Asher Lev* (New York: Ballantine Books, 1973), 218.

21. Ibid., 313.

22. Ibid., 332.

23. Clifford Elliott, "Crucified Woman," 19-20.

24. In Gladys Gilkey Calkins, *Follow Those Women*, (New York: NCC, 1961), 6-7.

25. In Edwina Hunter, "Reflections on the *Christa*," in the *Journal of Women and Religion*, Vol. 4, No. 2 (Winter 1985): 25.

26. In *On the Prescription of Heretics*, 41.

27. See Karl Barth, *Church Dogmatics*, III/4.

28. Rosemary Radford Reuther,*Sexism and God-talk: Toward a Feminist Theology* (Boston: Beacon Press, 1983), 138.

29. Margaret Randall, *Sandino's Daughters* (Vancouver: New Star Books, 1981), 48-49.

30. Douglas John Hall, *God and Human Suffering* (Minneapolis: Augsburg Publishing House, 1986), 99.

31. *Globe and Mail*, 26 September 1990.

32. Read into the Debates of the Senate by Royce Firth, *Hansard*, Wednesday, February 21, 1990.

33. Michele Landsberg, *Toronto Star*, 8 December 1989. (Used by permission of Michele Landsberg/*Toronto Star*.)

34. *Toronto Star*, ibid.

35. See *Suffering*, 81.

36. *Confessions* 9.9.

37. Doris Lessing, *The Memoirs of a Survivor* (New York: Alfred A. Knopf, 1975), 168-169.

38. Alice Walker, *The Color Purple* (New York: Simon and Schuster, Inc., 1982), 178-179.

About the Artist

Almuth Lutkenhaus-Lackey was born in Germany and studied in the art colleges of Dortmund and Muenster. Over twenty of her life-size sculptures and larger-than-life-size sculptures and sculptured walls are to be found in public buildings and other locations in Germany.

Since coming to Canada in 1966, Almuth Lutkenhaus-Lackey has received many commissions. Her sculptures can be found in Toronto, Ottawa, Windsor, Belleville, Brantford, Burlington, Oakville, Waterloo, and Trois Rivières.

Her many one-woman shows have included retrospectives in Germany and in Ottawa, at the National Arts Centre. At the invitation of the Canadian Embassy in Germany she represented Canada in the "Bundesquartenschau" at Bonn.

Many public collections in Canada and Germany include one or more of her sculptures. Lutkenhaus has portrait busts of Robertson Davies and Dorothy Livesay, at Massey College and at Trinity College of the University of Toronto, respectively. Her bust of Margaret Laurence is at Trent University, Peterborough; a bust of ballet dancers Karen Kain and Frank

Augustyn is in the lobby of the O'Keefe Centre in Toronto; a bust of Celia Franca is in the Art Gallery of Ontario; and a bust of Barker Fairley is in the National Library in Ottawa. The Lutkenhaus sculpture commissioned by Dr. M. Cowpland of Ottawa, called *Solstice* (seven meter gold and bronze), will be moved to the Museum of Civilization in 1991. She was sculptor-in-residence at the Ottawa School of Art from 1981 to 1985.

Lutkenhaus-Lackey has won many awards and grants in both Germany and Canada. In Germany, she was awarded the first prize at Landemuseum Muenster; the Medal of Honour from the city at Hamm, and the Silver Needle from Salzburg. The International Zonta Club named her "Woman of the Month of October" in 1976. A jury composed of Pierre Berton, Jack Pollock, and A.Y. Jackson awarded her Best Sculpture of the Autumn Festival of the Arts in Toronto in 1969. She received five grants from the Ontario Arts Council for "Creative Artists in Schools," and three grants for "Individual Artists." Her work has been shown in many locations in Ontario including the 1988 National Society of Canadian Sculptors show in the Toronto City Hall. She was one of the organizers and participants in the first Christian Festival in Ottawa in 1982, where the sculpture *Crucified Woman* was exhibited.

Since 1983 Lutkenhaus-Lackey has been very ill and has turned to painting, as she can no longer sculpt. She has had a one-woman show of her paintings in Ottawa and has participated in the Arts Credo show in Toronto.

Lutkenhaus-Lackey lives with her husband Arthur Lackey in Ottawa. She has two daughters, one living in Canada and one in Germany. She also has grandchildren, many friends, and keeps in touch with her many former students. Lutkenhaus-Lackey is a member of the Anglican Church of Canada.

About the Author

Doris Jean Dyke is a professor at Emmanuel College of Victoria University in the University of Toronto. Emmanuel College is a theological college of The United Church of Canada.

Professor Dyke began teaching at Emmanuel in 1977, the first woman to hold a professorial appointment in a United Church theological college in Canada. Her teaching includes courses in the educational ministry of the church, ministry and feminism, and faith and the arts.

She was born Doris Jean Scott and grew up on a farm near Toronto. Her first career was as a primary school teacher. She was among the first teachers to be granted maternity leave when her daughter Catherine was born in the fifties. Her husband Oswald Dyke died in 1959, and she and her daughter moved to New York City where she began graduate studies.

Professor Dyke holds an undergraduate degree from Queen's University in Kingston, an undergraduate and master's degree from the University of Toronto, a master's degree from Columbia University, and a doctoral degree in religious education from Columbia and Union Theological Seminary.

After leaving New York in 1964, Professor Dyke moved to Saskatoon, where she taught philosophy of education at the University of Saskatchewan. She later became head of the Department of Educational Foundations. While in Saskatoon Professor Dyke adopted two children, Brenda and Tanya.

The Dyke family travelled extensively and moved a number of times. In addition to summers spent teaching in Calgary and Vancouver, there was a three-month stay in Cuernavaca, Mexico, and a full year in Louisville, Kentucky. In 1973, the family moved to Halifax where Professor Dyke was appointed Dean of Education at Dalhousie University. She has attended conferences in North America, Europe, Africa, and Asia and has undertaken educational travel in Canada, the United States, the United Kingdom, Nicaragua, India, the Philippines, Hong Kong, and U.S.S.R.

Professor Dyke has presented numerous papers, published articles, appeared on television, and given radio broadcasts in the fields of education, feminist theology, and theology and the arts. She has been active in inter-faith dialogue. In 1989, she received a senior research award from the Association of Theological Schools of the United States and Canada for her work on women and theology.

She is married to the Reverend Donald Milne. In the fall semester of 1989, they resided in Washington D.C., as visitors of Wesley Theological Seminary.

Printed in Canada

910111